WORLD RELIGIONS

PROTESTANTISM
THIRD EDITION

WORLD RELIGIONS

African Traditional Religion
Baha'i Faith
Buddhism
Catholicism & Orthodox Christianity
Confucianism
Daoism
Hinduism
Islam
Judaism
Native American Religions
Protestantism
Shinto
Sikhism
Zoroastrianism

WORLD RELIGIONS

PROTESTANTISM
THIRD EDITION

by
Stephen F. Brown
Series Editors: Joanne O'Brien and Martin Palmer

CHELSEA HOUSE
PUBLISHERS

An imprint of Infobase Publishing

Protestantism, Third Edition

Copyright © 2009, 2006, 2002 by Infobase Publishing

Chelsea House
An imprint of Infobase Publishing
132 West 31st Street
New York NY 10001

Library of Congress Cataloging-in-Publication Data
Brown, Stephen F.
  Protestantism / by Stephen F. Brown. — 3rd ed.
      p. cm. — (World religions)
  Includes bibliographical references and index.
  ISBN 978-1-60413-112-3
  1. Protestantism—Juvenile literature. I. Title.
  BX4805.3.B76 2009
  280'.4—dc22

            2008029659

Chelsea House books are available at special discounts when purchased in bulk quantities for businesses, associations, institutions, or sales promotions. Please call our Special Sales Department in New York at (212) 967-8800 or (800) 322-8755.

You can find Chelsea House on the World Wide Web at http://www.chelseahouse.com

This book was produced for Chelsea House by Bender Richardson White, Uxbridge, U.K.
Project Editor: Lionel Bender
Text Editors: Ronne Randall and Cathy Meeus
Designer: Ben White
Picture Researchers: Joanne O'Brien and Kim Richardson
Maps and symbols: Stefan Chabluk

Printed in China

CP BRW 10 9 8 7 6 5 4 3 2 1
This book is printed on acid-free paper.

All links and Web addresses were checked and verified to be correct at the time of publication. Because of the dynamic nature of the Web, some addresses and links may have changed since publication and may no longer be valid.

CONTENTS

PREFACE

Almost from the start of civilization, more than 10,000 years ago, religion has shaped human history. Today, more than half the world's population practice a major religion or indigenous spiritual tradition. In many 21st-century societies, including the United States, religion still shapes people's lives and plays a key role in politics and culture. And in societies throughout the world increasing ethnic and cultural diversity has led to a variety of religions being practiced side-by-side. This makes it vital that we understand as much as we can about the world's religions.

The World Religions series, of which this book is a part, sets out to achieve this aim. It is written and designed to appeal to both students and general readers. The books offer clear, accessible overviews of the major religious traditions and institutions of our time. Each volume in the series describes where a particular religion is practiced, its origins and history, its central beliefs and important rituals, and its contributions to world civilization. Carefully chosen photographs complement the text, and sidebars, a map, fact file, glossary, bibliography, and an index are included to help readers gain a more complete understanding of the subject.

These books will help clarify what religion is all about and reveal both the similarities and differences in the great spiritual traditions practiced around the world today.

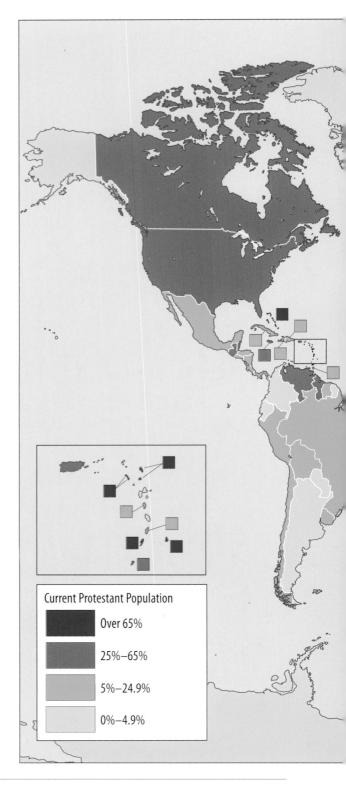

Current Protestant Population

- Over 65%
- 25%–65%
- 5%–24.9%
- 0%–4.9%

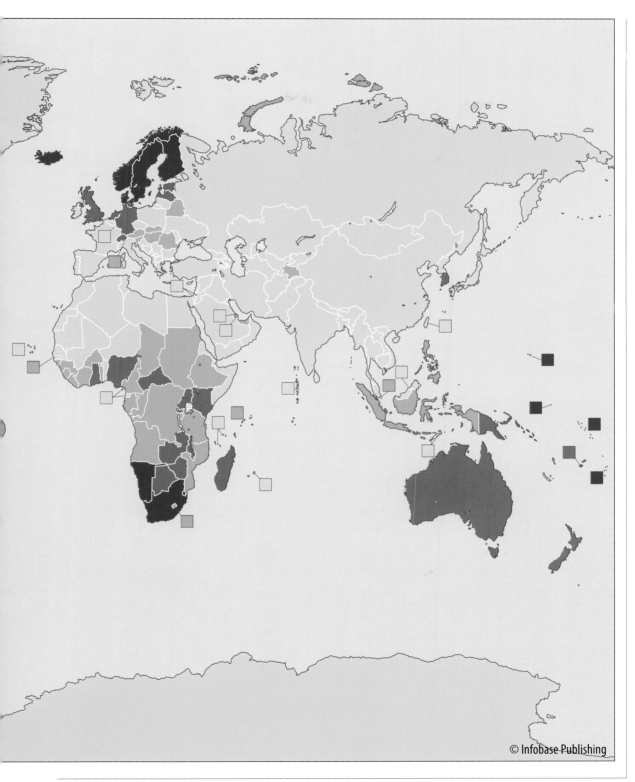

© Infobase Publishing

CHAPTER 1

INTRODUCTION: THE PROTESTANT WORLD

North America is a predominantly Christian continent. In fact people born in present-day North America would find it hard to avoid the influence of the Christian religion. For example, the year they were born would be the Year of Our Lord (Anno Domini, or A.D., but now referred to as Common Era, C.E.) 1960, or 1980, or 2000. Christmas, which celebrates Jesus Christ's birth, and Easter, which celebrates his rising from the dead, are noted on calendars across America. On a drive through almost any city or town in the United States or Canada, one is likely to see a high-steepled church in the center of town or a simple meeting hall for Christian prayer. Turning on a television or a radio on any Sunday morning one can hear a preacher, a gospel singer, or a harmonious choir.

American history and culture have been shaped by Christianity in many ways. And the rich diversity of Christian faith is well suited for a nation of diverse peoples and traditions. The Protestant branches of Christianity illustrate this diversity very well. Whereas Roman Catholic Christianity is known for its unity

Methodist minister blessing the bread and wine on the altar during a communion service.

Many Protestant churches in small towns and throughout rural areas in the United States and Canada are large bright halls of worship and prayer that focus on the study and preaching of the Bible.

under the pope and its long historical religious tradition, Protestant Christianity is renowned for its different forms and renewals of religious practice.

Protestant Christians, all united in their faith in Christ, manifest their religious differences in diverse ways: through the religious community's type of leadership, through the diversity of their basic beliefs, or through their manner of worship. Protestant churches in your area might be called Saint Mary's Episcopal Church, Resurrection Lutheran Church, or Calvary United Methodist Church. The notice board in front of a humble prayer hall might read Middletown Believers Fellowship, The Evangelical Friends Church, or The Standard Church.

The Protestant religious melting pot in the United States is not just a product of English, Scottish, and German immigrants. It consists of hundreds of Christian communities, some home-grown, some imported: Episcopalians, Lutherans, Presbyterians, Christian Scientists, Jehovah's Witnesses, and Mormons. It is a melting pot of people from Sweden and Holland, Jamaica and South Africa, Korea and Australia. As such it is a true reflection of the sheer scale and diversity of Protestantism worldwide

THE BROAD NATURE OF PROTESTANT UNIVERSALITY

Protestantism is by its very nature a missionary faith. It arose in Europe as a protest (hence Protestant) against the corruption of the Catholic Church and as such it had to try and win converts. This missionary zeal, initially directed at the already Christian communities of Europe, later led Protestants to launch major missionary movements, such as the Society for the Propagation of Christian Knowledge founded in the late 17th century to evangelize Native peoples in North America, or the Methodist Missionary Society founded at the end of the 18th century to spread Protestantism to Africa.

It is in the nature of protesters that they fall out with each other—and Protestants prove this point. Every since the first challenge to the power of the Catholic Church by Martin Luther in the early part of the 16th century, the Protestant movement has splintered into competing churches. It is now estimated that there are more than 50,000 different Protestant groups worldwide. This has ensured a missionary drive within Protestantism as competing groups tried to win more souls than their rivals.

Missionaries spread throughout the world in the 19th century. All over Africa, Asia, and the Americas, Protestant groups were created and peoples converted—some very successfully as, for example, in such countries as Kenya and Uganda, others not so

Christians gathered at a small community church named The Tree of Life in a town in South Africa.

successfully as, for instance, in China. The result is that there are Protestant churches in every country, each with their own distinct traditions and practices.

Migration has meant that almost all of these churches are now present in the United States, often continuing their traditional practices but also at the same time, learning to meld into the general Protestant background of the States.

A DIFFERENT WAY OF BEING CHRISTIAN

Protestantism is more than just a collection of different churches. It is also a way of being Christian that is rooted in a personal relationship with God through Jesus Christ, and differs from the Catholic and Orthodox ways because Protestants do not need a priest to be the mediator. This has led to a strong personal ethical stance within Protestantism because Protestants believe that when they die they must be personally responsible for all their actions before God. This strong ethical and moral dimension has meant that many social reform movements—from abolition of slavery to environmental action—have been spearheaded by Protestants.

WORLDWIDE CHRISTIANITY

The extension of the Christian religion from the lands surrounding the Mediterranean Sea to every region of the world has taken many centuries, and in East Asia and in Muslim territories its presence remains very small. Nevertheless, out of the rough total of 6.5 billion people in the world, more than 2.1 billion—almost 33 percent of the world's population—are Christians. Of these an estimated 750 million people are members of the many different Protestant communities.

Protestantism also places a major responsibility upon its followers to live worthy lives. This has meant earning your own keep; working hard; working well. This is often called the Protestant Work Ethic and is seen to lie behind the industrial and commercial success of the United States.

Faith was meant by Christianity's founder to become part of every aspect of a believer's life. Therefore it is not surprising that Reverend Martin Luther King Jr. (1929–68) led marches of Christians from every denomination for civil rights in the southern United States during the 1950s and 1960s. Neither is it unusual today for a Catholic or Protestant baseball player to make the sign of the cross before stepping to the plate, or pointing to heaven after hitting a home run; or for a football star to kneel for a short, silent prayer of thanksgiving after scoring a touchdown. Nor is it strange to visit a beloved sick relative at hospitals with names like Deaconess Hospital, New England Baptist Hospital, or Good Samaritan Hospital. It is almost expected that a soup kitchen for the poor or the homeless will be run by a church group. And paging through the phone book, one finds dozens of listings under the heading Social Services that reflect Protestant origins.

WORLDWIDE SOCIAL ACTION

All these activities of the Christian faith are specially highlighted in Protestant churches, and illustrate Christianity's vital presence not just in the United States, or indeed even in "Christian" countries such as Italy or the United

Charitable Deeds

Following Jesus Christ in acts of charity and goodwill is based on the account of the Final Judgment in chapter 25 of the gospel of Saint Matthew:

Then the King will say to those on His right hand, "Come, you blessed of My Father, inherit the kingdom prepared for you from the foundation of the world: for I was hungry and you gave Me food; I was thirsty and you gave Me drink; I was a stranger and you took Me in; I was naked and you clothed Me; I was sick and you visited Me; I was in prison and you came to Me." Then the righteous will answer Him, saying, "Lord, when did we see You hungry and feed You, or thirsty and give You drink? When did we see You a stranger and take You in, or naked and clothe You? Or when did we see You sick, or in prison, and come to You?" And the King will answer and say to them, "Assuredly, I say to you, inasmuch as you did it to one of the least of these My brethren, you did it to Me."

—Genesis 12:1–3

ARCHBISHOP DESMOND TUTU

The self-sacrificing character of Jesus Christ's message can be seen in the tireless efforts of Christians around the world. Archbishop Desmond Tutu (1931–), an Anglican cleric known for his courageous efforts to improve the lot of black South Africans, has been celebrated with the 1984 Nobel Prize for Peace. Many of his sermons and speeches as bishop of Lesotho and general secretary of the South African Council of Churches have been published in his books *Hope and Suffering, Crying in the Wilderness,* and *The Rainbow People of God: The Making of a Peaceful Revolution* (written with John Allen).

Widely viewed as South Africa's "moral conscience," Desmond Tutu, former archbishop of Cape Town, has worked tirelessly for peace and reconciliation in his native land.

Kingdom, but throughout the world. Christianity and especially Protestant Christianity is to be found in many areas of human endeavor—fighting for justice, healing the sick, clothing and feeding the poor, and visiting the imprisoned. Traditionally these activities are the Christian works of mercy: Feed the hungry, give drink to those who are thirsty, clothe the naked, shelter the homeless, care for the sick, and bury the dead. In all these acts of charity and goodwill Protestants believe that they see Jesus Christ himself in the neighbor whom they help.

CONTINUING TRADITIONS

Many of the missions Americans assign to Protestant churches and institutions are part of what they inherited from western Europe or their other countries of origin. When Anglicans who came from England in the 18th century arrived here they discovered churches that made them feel at home. The religious services were the same as in their homeland, and so were the hymns and many of the social activities. If their Episcopalian descendants returned to England today they would not feel like strangers in local Anglican parishes.

The children of Lutherans who came from Germany were introduced to their religious traditions by the guidance of the General Synod, the General Council, and the United Synod South, which were fused into the United Lutheran Church in 1918. Lutherans today would feel quite comfortable if they returned to an Evangelical church in the Germany of their ancestors.

Today, Christians arriving from Iraq will find that their ancient Church is well represented and people from, for example, Nigeria will find flourishing churches that have been brought to the United States by earlier Nigerian immigrants.

PROTESTANT INFLUENCE ON EDUCATION

In the lands from which American immigrants came great emphasis was placed on education. Followers of Martin Luther (1483–1546) brought into existence strong educational programs and university courses that still play a large part in

Founded by the Congregational Church in 1636, Harvard
University is a product of the commitment to education of the
Protestants who settled in New England in the 17th century.
It still maintains its strong Christian traditions.

EARLY COLLEGES AND UNIVERSITIES FOUNDED BY THE CONGREGATIONAL CHURCH

1636 Harvard University
1701 Yale University
1769 Dartmouth University
1793 Williams College
1794 Bowdoin College
1800 Middlebury College
1821 Amherst College
1829 Illinois College
1833 Oberlin College
1835 Marietta College
1837 Knox College
1837 Mount Holyoke College
1844 Olivet College
1846 Beloit College
1846 Grinnell College
1847 Rockford College

German education. John Knox (ca. 1514–72) set high ideals for a comprehensive system of education that has strongly influenced Scotland and the Presbyterian Church. American Protestants retained that tradition.

For the most part, American Protestants attended and supported the public schools for primary and secondary education since they could often depend on their majority to influence school teaching policies. The case was different at the higher levels of education. Some of America's oldest and most highly regarded universities, such as Harvard and Yale, have religious origins. Duke, Emory, and Southern Methodist in the South; Boston University and Wesleyan in the Northeast; Earlham and Wheaton in the Midwest; and Brigham Young and Pepperdine in the West all have Protestant roots, and some still attempt to preserve their church tradition, even if in many cases it might be limited to their schools of divinity.

THE PROTESTANT LIFE OF FAITH: PRAYER AND WORSHIP

For Protestant Christians all these visible activities that bear witness to Christianity's fruitfulness in today's world only have worth when they are performed out of love for God and one's neighbor. They are acts of praise to God for the glories of his creation, or acts of thanksgiving for God's benefits, or acts of love attempting to respond to the love that God has shown to humankind, when, according to Christian belief, God's son "became flesh and dwelt among us." (John 1:14) The center of Protestant life is not so much these activities themselves as the life of prayer and worship that inspires Christians in all areas of human endeavor.

Following the Path of Christ

As Protestants live their lives, they operate under the guidance of Christ and often recite Psalm 23:

The Lord is my shepherd;
I shall not want.
He makes me to lie down in green
pastures;
He leads me beside the still waters.
He restores my soul;
He leads me in the paths of righteousness
For His name's sake.
Yea, though I walk through the valley of
the shadow of death,
I will fear no evil;
For You are with me;
Your rod and Your staff, they comfort me.
You prepare a table before me in the
presence of my enemies;
You anoint my head with oil;
My cup runs over.
Surely goodness and mercy shall
follow me
All the days of my life;
And I will dwell in the house
of the Lord, Forever.

—Psalm 23

The Protestant life of prayer and worship is shown in the high ceremonies of an Episcopalian Mass, in the choruses of the Mormon Tabernacle Choir, in the prayer services of the Methodist minister reciting a psalm, in the vibrant "Amens" of the Pentecostals, and in the quiet sittings of the Quakers. Protestant faith has many voices and faces.

CHAPTER 2

THE ORIGINS OF PROTESTANTISM

All branches of Christianity (Catholic, Orthodox, and Protestant) claim a common origin from Jesus Christ. Jesus, according to the Christian scriptures, established a new covenant between God and his chosen people. The New Covenant continues and completes the Old Covenant God made with the Jewish people.

Matthew's Gospel is associated with the early Jewish Christian community. It introduces the reader to how the early Christian church in Jerusalem and its environs believed that Jesus brought a New Law that complemented the Old Law. It also explains how Jesus was the Messiah, or the anointed king, promised to the Jewish people. While presenting the differences between the Old Law and the New Law, this Gospel also attempts to show how Jesus Christ continues the spirit of the Jewish law and fulfills the promises of the prophets. Matthew's Gospel thus cannot be completely understood without a knowledge of Judaism; nor can Christianity.

A father and his daughters in prayer. Prayers may be read from a book, spoken, or recited in silence, and are said kneeling, sitting, or standing.

THE CHOSEN PEOPLE

To appreciate the Gospel of Matthew, then, one must go back to the beginning of God's plan as Christians understand it; one must go back to the Jewish scriptures. According to the first book of the Jewish scriptures, Genesis, the Jewish people descended from a wandering herdsman, Abraham, who left Ur in Babylonia and under God's guidance headed toward a land that God promised him and his offspring. Through Abraham the Lord God made

THE TEN COMMANDMENTS

According to Exodus, the second book of the Bible, God renewed his agreement with the descendants of Abraham. He did so by giving Moses and his people the Ten Commandments and other laws. These commandments gave more specific directions to the Jewish people, telling them what God expected of his chosen ones. By following these commandments they showed that they were God's faithful people.

I. *I am the Lord your God, who brought you out of the land of Egypt, out of the house of bondage. You shall have no other gods before me.*

II. *You shall not take the name of the Lord your God in vain.*

III. *Observe the Sabbath day, to keep it holy.*

IV. *Honor your father and your mother.*

V. *You shall not murder.*

VI. *You shall not commit adultery.*

VII. *You shall not steal.*

VIII. *You shall not bear false witness against your neighbor.*

IX. *You shall not covet your neighbor's wife.*

X. *You shall not covet your neighbor's house, his field . . . or anything that is your neighbor's.*

—Deuteronomy 5:6–21

a covenant with his chosen people. He promised that he would watch over them, that they would be his people, and that they would become a great nation. He also expected that, on their part, they would live as he expected and that they would give their neighbors an example of how God wanted all men to live.

THE COMING OF A SAVIOR

According to Jewish accounts, God's chosen people entered the Promised Land. Over time they created kings; David and Solomon were the most famous. The kingdom, however, later split into two parts: Israel and Judah. Each of these kingdoms in turn was captured by the Assyrians and the Babylonians. The descendants of Abraham and David then frequently found themselves dominated by foreign nations.

These various captivities helped build among the Jewish people a hope for a new leader who might free them from slavery. In these struggling years before Jesus Christ's birth, the prophets, starting with Isaiah, foretold the coming of a Messiah, a savior who would redeem his people and restore the kingdom of God. The Messiah was pictured in different ways by Jewish writers: Some thought he would return as a military leader overthrowing their oppressors; others expected him to be a great teacher; still others imagined him, according to the prophecy of Jeremiah, as a suffering servant. Matthew's Gospel presents Jesus Christ as a descendant of Abraham and David. Jesus is thus portrayed, like Abraham, as one from whom a great nation would descend. He was also, like David, a king who could lead his people. The very beginning of this Gospel, then, recalls the hopes held so high among the oppressed Jewish people. It was during these days of high hopes for a Messiah that a man began to go among the Jewish people and preach about the coming of the kingdom of heaven:

The kingdom of heaven is like a mustard seed, which a man took and sowed in his field, which indeed is the least of all the seeds; but when it is grown it is greater than the herbs and becomes a tree, so that the birds of the air come and nest in its branches. —Matthew 13:31–32

Some saw this wandering preacher as merely another rabbi, or teacher, who spent his days interpreting Jewish law. Others saw him as a leader in their fight against the tyranny of Roman rule. And some saw him as the Messiah, sent by God to deliver them. This man was named Jesus of Nazareth. The main source of information about his life is the Christian Bible's New Testament, especially the Gospels of Matthew, Mark, Luke, and John.

THE EARLY LIFE OF JESUS

Little is known about the childhood of Jesus. However, we can assume that, as was the custom of his time and place, he began to work alongside his father, Joseph, at an early age and learned the trade of carpentry. The only incident of Jesus' childhood that the Gospels record is his meeting with the rabbis in the Temple at Jerusalem when he was 12 years old. According to Luke, Jesus' knowledge and understanding of Jewish law astonished and impressed the rabbis.

Jesus' method of teaching was to talk to the people, especially the common people. He was a Jew preaching to other Jews. In the synagogue on the Sabbath, learned men were often called upon to speak during the service, and it is likely that this is where Jesus first began to preach, before the crowds who gathered to listen to him grew too large for the synagogue. As his following increased, he also taught in the Temple, on the streets and roads, by the sea, and in the countryside—wherever he could find people willing to listen to his message.

THE LORD'S PRAYER

Jesus Christ instructed the expectant Jewish people concerning the kingdom of his Father, and taught them to pray:

Our father in heaven,
Hallowed be Your name.
Your kingdom come.
Your will be done
On earth as it is in heaven.
Give us this day our daily bread.
And forgive us our debts,
As we forgive our debtors.
And do not lead us into
*   temptation,*
But deliver us from the evil one.
For Yours is the kingdom and the
*   power*
And the glory forever. Amen

—Matthew 6:9–13

THE PARABLES OF JESUS

Jesus taught by parables, or stories, that described ordinary situations in everyday life. He then drew out of these common instances a spiritual meaning. Parables generally have one point to make. The details of the story may or may not have a particular meaning. For instance, in the Gospel of Matthew, Jesus begins with this parable:

Behold, a sower went out to sow. And as he sowed, some seed fell by the wayside; and the birds came and devoured them. Some fell on stony

Part of a stained-glass window in Sainte-Chapelle in Paris, France. The images depict the story of a saint. The church was built in the 13th century to house what was believed to be Christ's crown of thorns and fragments of the wooden cross on which he was crucified.

MEANING OF THE PARABLES

The disciples of Jesus asked him why he spoke in parables. For example, what was the meaning of the parable of the seed-sower. Jesus explained:

Therefore, hear the parable of the sower: When anyone hears the word of the kingdom, and does not understand it, then the wicked one comes and snatches away what was sown in his heart. This is he who received seed by the wayside. But he who received the seed on stony places, this is he who hears the word and immediately receives it with joy; yet he has no root in himself, but endures only for a while. For when tribulation or persecution arises because of the word, immediately he stumbles. Now he who received seed among the thorns is he who hears the word, and the cares of this world and the deceitfulness of riches choke the word, and he becomes unfruitful. But he who received seed on the good ground is he who hears the word and understands it, who indeed bears fruit and produces: some a hundredfold, some sixty, some thirty.

—Matthew 13:18–23

places, where they did not have much earth; and they immediately sprang up because they had no depth of earth. But when the sun was up they were scorched, and because they had no root they withered away. And some fell among thorns, and the thorns sprang up and choked them. But others fell on good ground and yielded a crop: some a hundredfold, some sixty, some thirty. —Matthew 13:3–8

Parables give a vivid and memorable expression to a teacher's words and they also lead the listener to reflect on the teacher's words and take some responsibility for intepreting, accepting, or rejecting the message. The present parable would get people to ask themselves what kind of soil they had to offer for the planting of God's word. However, parables seem also to have another function. They allow the preacher to deal in a softer, more indirect way with a hostile audience. This appears to be the case with Jesus' parable of weeds mixed with the wheat. The primary point is that in life the wheat and the weeds, or the good and the bad, will always exist together:

The kingdom of heaven is like a man who sowed good seed in his field: but while men slept, his enemy came and sowed tares among the wheat and went his way. But when the grain had sprouted and produced a crop, then the tares also appeared. So, the servants of the owner came and said to him, "Sir, did you not sow good seed in your field? How then does it have tares?" He said, "An enemy has done this." The servants said to him, "Do you want us then to go and gather them up?" But he said, "No, lest while you gather up the tares, you

BOOKS OF THE NEW TESTAMENT

Gospels:
Matthew
Mark
Luke
John
Acts of the Apostles
Letters:
Romans
Corinthians 1 and 2
Galatians
Ephesians
Philippians

Colossians
Thessalonians 1 and 2
Timothy 1 and 2
Titus
Philemon
Hebrews
James
Peter 1 and 2
John 1, 2, and 3
Jude
Revelation

also uproot the wheat with them. Let both grow together until the harvest, and at the time of harvest I will say to the reapers, 'First gather together the tares and bind them in bundles to burn them, but gather the wheat into my barn.'" —Matthew 13:24–30

It would not be hard to imagine that Jesus is speaking not only about the wheat and the weeds, but also about those who are sowing the weeds—those rejecting his message and undermining his divine mission. In other words, in speaking about the enemy that sows the tares among the grain, Jesus lets us know that his message is not acceptable to everyone.

THE MESSAGE OF JESUS

Jesus taught that salvation depends on true devotion to the will of God, not merely following the letter of religious law. In his sermons and parables, or stories that illustrate religious principles, Jesus drew from Judaic tradition the message of love and forgiveness that he preached, but he gave new meaning to this tradition. The striking difference between his teachings and the teachings of Judaism was his emphasis on love as opposed to law. Jesus called people away from the letter of the Jewish law to its spirit. He did not think that he was overthrowing Judaic law. He said, "Do not think that I came to destroy the Law or the Prophets. I did not come to destroy but to fulfill." (Matthew 5:17) Nevertheless his teachings created enemies among the Jewish religious leaders whose authority his message was undermining. Meanwhile he was growing into a Jewish leader with a large following.

A drawing of Christ teaching from an illustrated 19th-century Ethiopian Bible.

JESUS AS THE NEW LAWGIVER

In Chapter 5 of his Gospel, Matthew recounts Jesus' Sermon on the Mount. This sermon, like Moses' reception of the Ten Commandments, takes place on a mountain. It provides the teachings of the New Law, or Covenant.

Moses, according to Matthew's account, had received the Old Law from God; Jesus proclaimed the New Law as God: "You have heard that it was said . . . but I say to you . . . Take heed that you do not do your charitable deeds before men, to be seen by them . . . And when you pray, you shall not be like the hypocrites . . ." (Matthew 5:20–6.5)

CHALLENGERS TO THE NEW LAW

Who were Matthew's "hypocrites?" Who were Christ's challengers among the Jews? The Gospel account speaks generally of

THE SERMON ON THE MOUNT

Jesus gave the teachings of this New Law or Covenant through this sermon.

Blessed are the poor in spirit, for theirs is the kingdom of heaven. Blessed are those who mourn, for they shall be comforted. Blessed are the meek, for they shall inherit the earth. Blessed are those who hunger and thirst for righteousness, for they shall be filled. Blessed are the merciful, for they shall obtain mercy. Blessed are the pure in heart, for they shall see God. Blessed are the peacemakers, for they shall be called sons of God. Blessed are those who are persecuted for righteousness' sake, for theirs is the kingdom of God.

—Matthew 5:3–10

Jesus then goes on to compare the Law and the Gospel teachings:

For I say to you, that unless your righteousness exceeds the righteousness of the scribes and Pharisees, you will by no means enter the kingdom of heaven.

—Matthew 5:20

three kinds of opponents to the message of Christ: the scribes, the Sadducees, and the Pharisees.

THE SCRIBES

The word scribe means "writer." The Jewish scribes were not just writers of anything, but copiers of the Torah, or Jewish scriptures. Since writers are frequently also readers, the scribes were close readers of the Hebrew text of the scriptures and were the official expounders of its meanings. Whereas the function of priests was to care for ceremonies, the function of the scribes was to clarify doctrine and teaching. The priests would certainly suspect anyone who was not trained by them to be a true interpreter of the Torah or the Old Law. Even more, the Mosaic Law was a divinely given law. A person who would offer a New Law, and do so in his own name, would in the view of the scribes be challenging God himself and God's law. The scribes had, therefore, many reasons to challenge Jesus and his message.

THE SADDUCEES

The Sadducees gained influence in Judea when Rome ruled. They gained their strength by anchoring themselves and the Jewish community in the Jewish tradition. Remembering the Assyrian Captivity that began in 731 B.C.E. when the Jewish people were dispersed and became weak and splintered, the Sadducees searched for a way to preserve this identity.

During the time of their captivity the Jewish people had intermarried and lost their identity as God's chosen people. The Sadducees thought to preserve the identity of the Jewish people through a loyal attachment to the original law—the Torah, or first five books of the Old Testament. Tradition begot security. Christ, as a person who was challenging tradition, was seen as an opponent who raised suspicion and concern.

THE PHARISEES

The Pharisees received their name from the Hebrew word for "separatists." The Pharisees helped to develop an elaborate system of oral laws added to the written law of Moses. They were separatists from the Sadducees. Through these laws the Pharisees sought to adjust Jewish life to the new circumstances and give concrete directives in a changing world.

The Pharisees had some special teachings that showed their adaptation to new circumstances. They began to speak of immortality, or life after death, which put them in opposition to the Sadducees, who denied an afterlife. There are ways in which Jesus might be considered a Pharisee: He was developing a New Law. Yet his radical claims were more than mere adaptation to circumstances. He was claiming to present a completely New Law. He was challenging the whole view of Law as fulfilling obligations. He was pushing to a more spiritual level that set the Old Law's list of required actions aside.

Christ's New Law was more radical than any of these groups could accept. He was, in their views, not just adapting the Law. He was giving a New Law that was not a law at all. His message was a message that transcended this world and pointed to a very different Promised Land. It seemed otherworldly and adverse to Jewish tradition.

JESUS' DEATH ON THE CROSS

In the spring of the third year of his preaching ministry, Jesus traveled from Galilee to Jerusalem for Passover. According to Matthew's Gospel (21:8–11) his entry into the city was triumphal, with crowds of people proclaiming him the Messiah. In the traditional Eastern manner, many honored him by throwing their cloaks in front of him; others cut branches from trees and strewed them in his path; and others shouted joyous hosannas acclaiming him.

As soon as Jesus' triumphal entry into Jerusalem became known to the priests of the Temple, they began plotting against him. Jesus' greatest enemies were the Pharisees and scribes. These religious leaders demanded that people conform not only to the written Law as handed down by Moses but also to the developed oral tradition that interpreted it and gave it concrete applications and obligations. Jesus' readiness at times to disregard ceremonial rules in order to give more consideration to human needs and suffering challenged their way of life. They became actively hostile toward him.

THE LAST SUPPER

The night before the beginning of Passover Jesus and his 12 disciples gathered in the house of one of his followers to have supper together. It was at this meal that Jesus spoke the words that serve as the basis for the Christian sacrament of Holy Eucharist, or Communion, in which bread and wine are partaken of in commemoration of the death of Christ. Jesus took bread and when he had given thanks, broke it and shared it with his disciples, saying, "Take, eat; this is My body which is broken for you;

Leonardo da Vinci's *The Last Supper* portrays Jesus Christ's final meal with his disciples before his crucifixion and death.

do this in remembrance of Me." In the same manner he also took the cup after supper, saying, 'This cup is the new covenant in My blood. This do, as often as you drink it, in remembrance of Me." (1 Corinthians 11:24–25)

JESUS BETRAYED AND CONDEMNED TO DEATH

After the Last Supper, Jesus withdrew into a garden called Gethsemane, where he often went for prayer and meditation. His disciples went with him, except for Judas, who had left them earlier in the evening. As his disciples slept around him Jesus prayed. The silence of the garden was suddenly broken by the arrival of Judas leading a band of Roman soldiers and Jewish Temple police. Identified by the betraying kiss of his disciple Judas, Jesus was arrested and brought before the Sanhedrin, the council of Jewish leaders.

After the trial, the Sanhedrin found Jesus guilty of blasphemy. By Roman law, however, the Sanhedrin could not put Jesus to death. In order to avoid arousing the anger of Jesus' followers and to ensure his death, they took him before Pontius Pilate, the Roman procurator, and charged him with blasphemy and with organizing a revolt against Rome.

Pilate found Jesus innocent of treason and wanted to set him free. The Pharisees, however, would not let Pilate release him. Perhaps in an attempt to stay out of the internal conflicts among the Jews, Pilate gave in and sentenced Jesus to death. As was the custom with all condemned criminals, Jesus was first scourged, or whipped, and the Roman soldiers placed a crown of thorns on his head, mocking the charge that he had proclaimed himself king of the Jews.

THE CRUCIFIXION

Crucifixion was the form of death reserved by the Romans for low criminals, slaves, and revolutionaries. After Jesus' death, however, his own followers believed that his crucifixion was not a sign of extreme wickedness, but the fulfillment of a prophecy of Isaiah that the Messiah would be "despised and rejected by men,

A painting of the crucifixion above an altar in a church in Stockholm, Sweden. A sign that
Pontius Pilate ordered nailed to Jesus' cross provided more fuel for the ridicule of those who
did not believe in Jesus as the Messiah: "Jesus of Nazareth, The King of the Jews,"
it said in Aramaic, Greek, and Latin.

a man of sorrows and acquainted with grief . . . . Surely He has borne our griefs and carried our sorrows. . . . He was wounded for our transgressions, He was bruised for our iniquities . . . and by His stripes we are healed." (Isaiah 53:3–6)

When the soldiers and the mob taunted the dying Jesus he whispered, "Father, forgive them, for they do not know what they do." (Luke 23:34) After hours of unbearable pain he cried out, "My God, my God, why have You forsaken Me?" (Matthew 27: 46) Then his head dropped onto his chest, and he expired.

A Roman officer reported to Pilate that Jesus was dead, and his body was turned over to one of his followers, Joseph of Arimathea, for burial. Jesus' body was wrapped in a linen shroud and placed in a tomb that was sealed with a rock.

THE RESURRECTION OF JESUS

According to Matthew's Gospel, on the third day after Jesus was crucified, Mary Magdalene and the other Mary, the mother of James and Joseph, went to look at the tomb. There was a violent earthquake and an angel spoke to the women: "Do not be afraid, for I know that you seek Jesus who was crucified. He is not here; for He is risen, as He said. Come, see the place where the Lord lay." (Matthew 28:5–6)

Later the Gospel says Christ appeared to the 11 disciples. He said to them: "All authority has been given to Me in heaven and on earth. Go therefore and make disciples of all the nations, baptizing them in the name of the Father and of the Son and of the Holy Spirit, teaching them to observe all things that I have commanded you; and lo, I am with you always, even to the end of the age." (Matthew 28:18–20) With these words the story of Jesus according to Matthew's Gospel ends. Yet according to Christian belief, Christ continued, and continues today, to live through the church to which he gave his name.

THE EARLY CHRISTIAN CHURCH

The first Christians were the disciples of Christ, the simple fishermen that he wanted to make "fishers of men." Their first "catch," according to the Acts of the Apostles, was the Jewish community that had heard him preach, had seen the wonders he performed, and saw in him a great prophet and yet more.

The early origins of the Christian church are hardly distinguishable from a special Jewish community. Many Jews saw Christ as a special rabbi, a special teacher. Only gradually did they come to believe that Christ was more than just a teacher and that he had a larger mission. At first they continued to perform all the Jewish rituals on the Sabbath. Little by little they reenacted the Passover meal, realizing that Christ had, by his death and resurrection, given it a new meaning. As the fuller meaning of Christ's life and teaching dawned on them, historians tell us, they gradually began to separate from the Temple and synagogue. It is the beginning stage of this development that is chronicled in the Gospel of Matthew; the actual separation took longer and varied in different communities as Jewish communities, and Christian communities with Jewish background, left Palestine and moved into the Greek world.

PAUL—APOSTLE TO THE GENTILES

Paul, a key writer of the New Testament, may have preached and written to the Hebrews, but it is not for that work that he is known. As he tells us in his Letter to the Galatians, a Gentile (non-Jewish) people to whom he had preached about Christ, he had been a very fervent Jew. He studied under the great rabbi Gamaliel. He even persecuted the Christians and was present at the death of the first Christian martyr, Saint Stephen. However, God brought him to a dramatic conversion, he claims, and Saul of Tarsus became Paul, a Jew who became an Apostle to the Gentiles. His letters to the many Christian communities show a man of tireless energy and daring adventures. His journeys are recounted in the Acts of the Apostles, Chapters 13–28.

PAUL'S LETTER TO THE GALATIANS

One of his most stirring letters is the Letter to the Galatians. It reveals the tensions of the early Christian church, so anchored in Jewish tradition and yet encountering a world that was not Jewish. Those Christians who favored a more Jewish form of Christianity had gone to Galatia to preach. According to them, to become a Christian one must first become circumcised like a Jew. In this Epistle Paul mocked these preachers, portraying them as preachers of "another gospel." If the Galatians followed these false preachers then faith in Christ and his redeeming sacrifice, Paul argued, was being betrayed in favor of salvation by following the demands of the Mosaic Law.

SEPARATION FROM MOSAIC LAW

For Paul it was no longer the Old Law that saved; it was faith in Christ's life and death that saved and brought to the Christian such fruits of faith as charity, joy, peace, patience, kindness, goodness, humility, self-control, and faithfulness itself. These are the gifts of the Spirit, Paul declares, that should direct their lives. They are not the results of following the Mosaic Law.

After much dispute with those who wanted to preserve the Christian ties with the Jewish tradition, Paul's argument triumphed over those who wanted to have a more Jewish form of Christianity. Thus Paul in his preaching to the Christian communities outside of Israel paved the road to a universal Christianity, free from the demands of the Mosaic Law.

FIRST CHRISTIAN COMMUNITIES

The early Christian church was a collection of communities descended from Christ's disciples. Early records have Christians gathering to commemorate the Lord's last supper, his death, and his resurrection. The historical records also have them sharing their goods in common. Many early documents also record local persecutions of the small communities of Christians and, later, the grander and more general perse-

Salvation Through Faith

Paul said that Christians are saved not through the Law, but through Jesus Christ:

"For I through the law died to the law that I might live to God. I have been crucified with Christ; it is no longer I who live, but Christ lives in me; and the life which I now live in the flesh I live by faith in the Son of God, who loved me and gave Himself for me."

—Galatians 2:19–20

cutions by the emperors, especially Decius (249–51) and Diocletian (284–305). More general persecutions indicate that Christian communities had grown appreciably and could be viewed as a serious, unified threat to the Roman Empire.

The emperor Constantine (306–37) saw in Christianity a movement that could bring a stronger unity to an empire that was splintering. For him it presented a moral ideal and a religious unity that could solidify his kingdom. Over time he made Christianity the official religion of the Roman Empire. At this point the Christian church gained its greatest respect and encountered its greatest temptation: to become a competing kingdom on earth.

An African wood-carving of Christ's crucifixion and Resurrection.

THE MESSAGE OF SAINT AUGUSTINE

Certainly this temptation was something to be resisted. This was the message of the fathers of the church, and especially the message of Saint Augustine, who wrote a monumental work, *The City of God*. Saint Augustine (354–430) lived at a crucial time in the history of the church and recognized that for a Christian the earthly city was not a lasting city.

He began his *Confessions* with the cry of his too-late-discovered awareness that "Thou has made us for thyself, O Lord, and our hearts are restless until they rest in Thee." People are restless, and according to Augustine they are looking for something more than the present life provides. They will find "peace" only when they have put their lives in place. He defines peace as "the tranquility of order." The order we search for is not to be found in ourselves. It can

Saint Augustine (354–430), bishop of Hippo, is the most influential writer of the Western church. His *Confessions* provide an account of the ascent of the ever-searching Christian to God. He said that God must be our highest interest, and when that is the case then the next in line is our soul, then our body, then external things. We attain peace, then, only when all things are in their proper place.

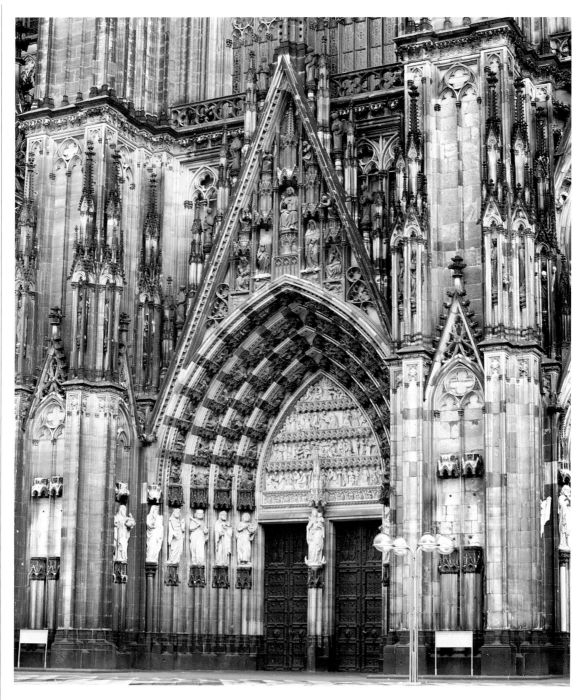

Cologne Cathedral in Germany. Work began on this Gothic church in 1248 and was finally completed in 1880. In medieval times the city of Cologne was also famous for its university, including the faculty of theology.

only be found if we arrive at the highest being (God), so that we may see how we and everything else fits in relation to God.

THE EARTHLY CITY AND THE HEAVENLY JERUSALEM

According to Augustine this should also be the model for society. The earthly city, whether of Rome or of any other earthly venue, can only attain peace when it is in the proper order with the heavenly Jerusalem, which literally means "city of peace." The proper order of political reality, then, demands that the earthly city be subordinated to the heavenly.

The earthly city is the means for arriving at the heavenly city. It provides or impedes the opportunity for gaining eternal happiness. The earthly city is important because it can lead us to our ultimate goal or away from it. It should be run, then, in a way that leads people to their ultimate heavenly goal. The emperor and his laws, and kings and their laws, must be subordinate to the laws that lead us to the things that are above.

THE MEDIEVAL PAPACY

Saint Augustine's view of the interconnection between the church and the state forms the foundation for the development of the papacy as the leading power in the Christian West. This development in the influence of the papacy took place over several centuries from Gregory I, or Gregory the Great (590–604), through Gregory VII (1073–85), Innocent III (1198–1216), to Boniface VIII (1294–1303) and beyond. According to the church, the end, or goal, of humanity is anchored beyond this world. This world, then, is the prelude to eternity. The path toward our ultimate goal is guided principally by the laws of the church. The laws of emperors or kings are important, but they have their legitimacy within the framework of a higher law, church law, and its goal, that of eternal life.

THE MEDIEVAL WORLD FROM A PROTESTANT VIEWPOINT

Compared with the portrait of the early church in the Acts of the Apostles, medieval Christianity offered a dramatic contrast. The simple gatherings of Christ's followers to commemorate his life and death had been replaced by formal ceremonies. Monasteries, whose monks were dedicated to a life of work and prayer and to the vows of poverty, chastity, and obedience, had become foundations supported by the wealthy and powerful, renowned for their grandeur and artistic treasures. As time went on the preachers of

The Abbey of Mont Saint-Michel in France. A church existed on this rock in the 10th century and over the following centuries further religious buildings were added. In medieval times Mont Saint-Michel was one of the major centers of pilgrimage in western Europe.

the gospel message were no longer simple fishermen; they were university professors like Saint Bonaventure and Saint Thomas Aquinas at Paris, and other figures at Oxford and Cologne, who brought their faculties great renown.

Theology, or the study of God, had become by the late 13th century a school discipline that attempted to compete with the learned studies of the Greek philosophers Aristotle and Plato. Its language was not that of the inspiring sermons of the fathers of the church but the technical language of logical, objective discourse. Popes were no longer the persecuted leaders of a minority religious faction; they were the equals of emperors. Medieval bishops at times seemed more involved with their prestige and the opportunity to move to a more important diocese than with the care of their flocks.

THE MEDIEVAL WORLD FROM A CATHOLIC VIEWPOINT

The medieval church was indeed organized and powerful. The papacy had over the years established an earthly city, the Church Militant, which aimed at leading its members to the heavenly Jerusalem (the Church Triumphant in union with God). However cities do not function without laws. The earthly city uses laws to attain its earthly goals. The church on earth also needs laws—laws that are different from earthly laws. Church laws must guide people to their heavenly home or goal. They are real and necessary, but have a higher goal that they are meant to aim at.

From the medieval viewpoint people need guidance, and laws are forms of guidance—prudent directives attempting to lead Christians to their final destiny—heaven.

Individuals—at least most individuals—cannot guide themselves. They are too hard at work making a living on earth to figure out the directions they should give their lives. For Christians this is why God gave his revelation. Revelation is humanity's guide to a higher life, for which the present life is a time of trial and preparation. However divine revelation itself is not clear for everyone. There is a need for wise readers and interpreters of God's will and design for humans. The popes and the Church provide this guidance much better than any king or emperor of the world could do, whose interests lie within this world.

Medieval universities built up outstanding faculties. Their professors were respected. Universities were founded in the Middle Ages to respond to the rediscovery of Aristotle's works and their translation into medieval university Latin.

THE CALL FOR REFORM IN THE CHURCH

Calls for the reform of Catholic practices were frequent in the Middle Ages. When monasteries became too tightly associated with the wealthy and influential, reformers called for a return to pure monastic discipline.

The reforms of Benedictine life in the 11th and 12th centuries at the newly established monasteries of Citeau and Cluny in France, the latter led by Bernard of Clairvaux (1090–1153), were very effective and caused true renewal. Abuses at the universities, where some professors seemed to have more academic respect for the sophistication of the Greek philosophy of Aristotle than they did for the simple parables of the Bible, were challenged by the condemnations of such thinking by the bishop of Paris in 1270 and 1277.

ABUSES IN WORSHIP

Further calls for reform in the 14th and 15th centuries were prompted by abuses in many other areas of church life. In the area of worship, for example, many Masses were said privately. This was censured as counter to the communal nature of Christian worship, since a priest takes the place of Christ who offered and continues to offer his sacrifice in the name of all. Many of the clergy also were ill trained; others were seriously violating their vows of celibacy; and bishops were often not residing in and caring for their dioceses.

The Great Western Schism between 1378 and 1417, with competing popes in Rome and Avignon, also caused confusion in church loyalties. There were many calls for the correction of these abuses.

SELLING INDULGENCES

One of the most serious abuses within the Catholic Church was in the area of the sale of indulgences. Indulgences are the remission of the temporal punishment due for the actual sins people commit. Pope Leo X (1475–1521) encouraged the preaching of indulgences in Germany to raise money for the rebuilding of Saint Peter's Basilica in Rome.

Johann Tetzel (1465–1519), a Dominican priest, preached for indulgences in a way that disturbed many. He declared that anyone who gave money to the rebuilding of Saint Peter's could choose a soul to be freed from purgatory. This manner of preaching indulgences would draw the accusation of "selling indulgences" and would become one of the chief abuses attacked by those clamoring for reforms within the church.

LUTHER'S CHALLENGE

In 1517 Martin Luther (1483–1546), a monk belonging to a Catholic religious order that associated itself with Saint Augustine, made two challenges to medieval Catholic traditions. In September Luther attacked a number of the teachings of medieval theologians. This first challenge drew small attention, since it could be understood only by those who were familiar with the subtle technicalities of theology. Less than two months later he criticized the preaching of indulgences and challenged especially the indulgence granted by Pope Leo X for those visiting and giving financial support to Saint Peter's Basilica in Rome.

This second form of criticism was much more widely understood and noted. Luther's challenges helped polarize other movements of criticism against the Roman

Indulgences: The Theory and Practice

Indulgences presuppose that the guilt of sins has been forgiven through the sacrament of penance and true contrition. Nonetheless sinners still owe some form of recompense for the offenses they have committed. Indulgences removed in full or in part this punishment due for sins. Indulgences could be obtained by certain kinds of prayer, by fasting, by giving alms, and by making pilgrimages. Indulgences could be gained for oneself or for others, especially for those who had died and were in purgatory awaiting liberation from the punishment as a result of their sins.

church. Princes and merchants who resented papal taxes or the pope's influence in local affairs welcomed Luther as a prophet of a new order. A number of priests and monks who were no longer dedicated to the practices of the priestly or religious life found in his criticisms a justification for deserting their monasteries and dioceses. Luther, without intending it, became the center of a major religious and social upheaval.

ORIGIN OF THE TERM *PROTESTANT*

The term *Protestant* arose a dozen years after Luther's first challenge, at the 1529 Diet, or lawmaking council, of Speyer, in Germany. Emperor Charles V (1519–56), in his effort to foster political unity to protect the Holy Roman Empire, a composite of lands in Germany and central Europe, against the threat of a Turkish invasion, limited Lutheran preaching to regions where the reform movement had already taken root. Five German Lutheran princes and the delegates from 14 Lutheran cities strongly protested this ruling. Thereafter the early Lutheran Reformation became associated with this minority "protest" movement.

A portrait of Charles V. He was the heir of four of Europe's leading dynasties of the 16th century — the Habsburgs of Austria, the Valois of Burgundy (now part of France and the Low Countries), the Trastamara of Castile, and the House of Aragon, both regions in Spain.

THE BASIC ISSUES

Reflections on the history leading up to the Reformation indicate that a definition of the Reformation is a complex issue. One becomes aware of this complexity in examining the term Protestant. It is a term that is very concrete historically. It shows the protest of Lutherans against Emperor Charles V's attempt to prevent the spread of their reform. However, many groups with different motives linked themselves to Luther's reform. The name Protestant absorbed all these various protests despite the fact that there was not a real unity of issues.

It is difficult, therefore, to identify all the issues that are associated with Protestantism. Yet it would be helpful to try to draw a picture of the main religious points of disagreement.

THE CATHOLIC VIEW OF THE CHURCH

In general the Catholic Church assumed that if it was to achieve its mission of leading its followers to eternal life, it had to involve itself with this world and had to attempt to direct it in a manner that would benefit Christians on their road to heaven. To attain the goal of assisting the wayfarer on his or her way of pursuing the road to their true homeland, the church needed power and influence over those who might direct them toward other goals. If the church did not take this lead, then earthly rulers would direct people through human laws to their own earthly goals. If the emperor or king became supreme, this might at times be spiritually beneficial. This would be the case if the emperor or king had a true Christian vision of life and its meaning and purpose. If, however, the ruler did not have a true Christian vision of things, then all the subjects would be led astray.

This basic Christian view of the primacy of the spiritual over the corporal, of the heavenly kingdom's superiority over the power of the earthly kingdom, of the primacy of religious authority over secular authority, had many repercussions. It gave a primacy to church law, church institutions, and church authority. It also made it difficult to raise objections against such laws, institutions, and authorities. If corruptions developed within these institutions, this was a situation that had to be accepted as a necessary part of reality.

THE PROTESTANT VIEW OF THE CHURCH

Protestants have varying attitudes toward the church. In general, though, they judge that a pope or a bishop or a priest is a man. He has all the limitations of any human. Just as an earthly ruler might lead his subjects astray, so may an ecclesiastical ruler. According to Protestants, people essentially are responsible for their own souls and their own spiritual health. They need God's grace, of course, since they cannot depend on laws and directives to get them to their eternal home. They say it is too easy to look for a magical way or set rituals to guarantee one's road to heaven.

The remains of Tintern Abbey in England, which was destroyed in 1539 during the Dissolution of the Monasteries. This was part of King Henry VIII's policy to establish control over the church in his realm.

To follow this path, however, is to return to the demands of the Mosaic Law from which Christ liberated humankind. Protestants say it is not institutions that save, it is Christ who saves. Rituals do not bring guarantees of spiritual benefit automatically. Therefore, Protestants say, indulgences too easily become forms of magic. So do repetitive actions that have been declared by church institutions to be the way to heaven. Religious faith should be trust in the power of Christ and the mercy of his heavenly father.

For Protestants Catholic religion had become routine and presumptive. It led people to go to Mass out of obligation, not out of a hope of joining in the thanksgiving that men owe to Christ as their Redeemer. Religion is a matter of the interior. It is an operation of the soul. Protestants say it is not a blind following of rules and repetitive rituals.

THE UNITY OF THE PROTESTANT REFORMATION

The chief characteristic of reform is always to stimulate other reforms. There are, in principle, so many things wrong, so many abuses to be corrected, so many bad practices to be improved that there is no end to efforts at reform. Because of this tendency to correct, any reformer will need to be corrected. This is part of the splintering process that has marked Protestantism. However, within each new reformation there is a continuing search for meaning that tends to keep Protestantism on track in an active pursuit of God.

CHAPTER 3

THE HISTORY OF PROTESTANTISM

The term Protestant arose from the protest made by some princes and town leaders at the Imperial Diet of Speyer in Germany in 1529. They protested the attempt by Emperor Charles V (1519–56) to limit the spread of Lutheranism. Soon people with other protests—against papal taxes, for example—allied themselves with the Lutheran cause. Over time, Protestant was the name given to any of the Western churches that separated themselves from the Catholic Church.

Many, however, think that the name Protestant carries a reactive connotation, suggesting a negative attitude toward the Catholic Church. They prefer to accentuate the positive spirit that characterized the Lutheran reform movement. They view Protestantism as a return to a more simple following of the Gospel. In their view the church began to compete with the empire for worldly power and prestige after it received recognition from Emperor Constantine. The building of the immense Lateran

Since it opened in 1912, the National Cathedral on Mount Saint Alban, Washington D.C. has been used for services with a national and ecumenical focus.

basilica was a sign of Constantine's largesse: It was bigger than any of the secular basilicas, or public meeting halls, in the Roman forum. It was to the simpler life of the early Christian church that the reformers wished to return.

THE CALL FOR REFORM

Every religious movement has to struggle with the issue of how spiritual and political power interact. How does the church relate to this world? Does it embrace it, condemn it, or compromise with it? How does God relate to the world? Does he work through intermediaries, like the pope and bishops, or does he interact directly with the souls of people themselves? Does God save people without their efforts? Or do people merit heaven? Stated more elaborately, is grace a quality that God gives to people that makes them holy? If this is the case, then when those who are in the state of grace do good acts, they perform acts that are meritorious—that is, acts that merit eternal life in heaven. Thus people who are filled with grace merit eternal life by their good acts. If, however, people are not holy, but are weak and corrupt, then their good works are useless. Such people thus do not merit eternal life. In their stead Christ merits eternal life for them. He alone saves. Which of these portraits of salvation is true?

THE NINETY-FIVE THESES

Martin Luther raised questions similar to these in the Ninety-five Theses, which he nailed to the door of the Wittenberg Castle Church on October 31, 1517. He set up a challenge against the Roman Catholic Church that contested its compromise with the political regimes and its strong affirmation of how good works rather than Christ alone merit humankind's salvation.

The religious world, for Luther, was more spiritual and less worldly. His basic premise, or proposition, was that religion should always be criticizing a cozy dependence on worldly things and earthly power. Since there would always be more things to criticize and correct, this would lead to more protesting against compromise and would demand further efforts at improvement,

The Wittenberg Castle Church is where Martin Luther nailed his Ninety-five Theses on October 31, 1517.

In his pamphlet "On Christian Liberty," Martin Luther explored the division between the political and the spiritual, the natural and the supernatural, by describing the hierarchy of popes and bishops as one imitating the grandeur of the kings and princes of this world. According to Luther, the church's position on merit by human efforts forced people to center their attention on themselves and to take pride in their own virtuous acts, rather than focusing on Christ as humanity's savior. The church's doctrine on indulgences, likewise, led people to think they could get to heaven by special human efforts—giving money to a designated cause, visiting certain churches, making special pilgrimages to special shrines—all external methods of achieving salvation through human endeavors rather than through Christ's sufferings and death.

very frequently with separating tendencies. For the first few decades of the reform movement, Ulrich Zwingli (1484–1531), Guillaume Farel (1489–1565), Martin Bucer (1491–1551), and John Calvin (1509–64), all took their turn at protesting and separating from the Catholic Church.

THE FIRST REFORMERS: LUTHER, ZWINGLI, AND CALVIN

A theologian, Martin Luther had challenged 97 theological theses on September 4, 1517, shortly before his more famous Wittenberg challenge against indulgences. The theological debates were more technical, and thus were lost on ordinary Christians. Indulgences had real meaning for believers, so Luther's debate shortly thereafter with Johann Tetzel, an indulgence preacher for Pope Leo X, drew attention. Those angry with the pope's interference in local affairs or with the taxes that they were forced to pay to Rome quickly linked themselves to Luther and his protests. When some of his followers began to condemn every aspect of the Catholic Church, Luther had to create a unified statement of reformed teachings to preserve his particular vision of reform. With the help of Philip Melanchthon (1497–1560), he wrote the Augsburg Confession of 1530 in an attempt to reconcile with moderate Catholics who might join them in their efforts to achieve reforms within the Catholic Church.

Ulrich Zwingli, however, opposed the Augsburg Confession. He declared that it compromised too much with Roman Catholicism. Zwingli was joined by the Sacramentarians who, like him, reduced the importance of the sacraments and denied the real presence of Christ in the Eucharist. Controversies over the

Martin Luther, the father of the Lutheran Church, called for dramatic reform within the Christian church and strongly criticized Catholicism.

sacraments became so intense that they caused a severe split between the more traditional Lutherans and the more radical Zwinglians. This was the first serious rift in Protestantism.

Martin Bucer, in Strasbourg, attempted to pull the reform movement back together again. He did not succeed but many of his ideas were picked up by John Calvin, who in his *Institutes of the Christian Religion* (1536) made a synthesis of the essential teachings of the reform movement that were midway between Luther and Zwingli. Calvin followed Luther in admitting Baptism and the Eucharist as sacraments, though in the case of the Eucharist he preferred to use the more biblical term *the Lord's Supper*. In a departure from Luther, however, he sided more with Zwingli when he attacked what he called the remaining sacraments as "false sacraments."

THE SPREAD OF PROTESTANTISM

The Lutheran reform movement progressed into northern Germany and then moved on to Denmark, Norway, Sweden, and present-day Finland. Zwingli's followers increased in numbers in Switzerland, the Austrian Tyrol, and also in Holland. Calvin's *Institutes* and his sermons formed the religious life of Protestant Geneva. By 1550 Calvinism was the strongest form of Protestantism, and Protestantism itself had spread over half of Europe. Calvinists carried their reform to parts of Switzerland, especially around Basel and Geneva. From there they spread to France and Holland. Through Calvin's disciple John Knox (1514–72) Calvinism was exported to Scotland and then to England, when Englishmen who were persecuted and exiled to Scotland by the Catholic queen, Mary Tudor (1553–58), returned home. Through emigration from their mother countries these various reforms and their offshoots were carried to the colonies in the United States.

THE REFORMATION IN ENGLAND

The Church of England broke with Rome when Henry VIII's (1491–1547) request for an annulment of his marriage to Catherine of Aragon was denied by Pope Clement VII (1523–34). In

1534 Parliament passed the Act of Supremacy, which established Henry as head of the church in England. While Henry himself remained basically a Catholic, Protestant reformers became more influential under his son, Edward VI (1537–53), and under Elizabeth I (1558–1603). The Thirty-nine Articles, approved by Parliament in 1571, established Anglicanism, a moderate form of Protestantism, as the official religion of England.

A CHURCH ANCHORED IN BELIEVERS

Right at the start of the English Reformation, the Bible translator William Tyndale (1492–1536) argued for a Church that was anchored in believers, as it is in the Bible, rather than in bishops. Tyndale so believed in what he considered the biblical portrait of the church that he translated the New Testament from Greek so that ordinary members of the church congregation could see the difference between the biblical church and the church that was the official Church in England. The English followers of John Calvin pushed for further reforms, attempting to "purify" the church even more. They wanted to restore it to the kind of Church that is represented by the Bible. This earned them the name *Puritans*. They principally opposed the episcopal (the bishops') dominance in the church and argued for the establishment of a church that respected the rights of local congregations. They soon became known as *Separatists* or *Congregationalists*.

PROTESTANTISM IN AMERICA

The Puritans or English Calvinists had tried to purify the English church. Those who judged that this effort bore little fruit decided to separate from the Church of England. These Separatists fled first to Holland in 1609. After a number of years they

John Milton

John Milton (1608–74), the English poet famous for his great epics *Paradise Lost* (1667) and *Paradise Regained* (1671), also was a Puritan, or English Calvinist, who continued the fight of the Puritans against the established Church of England. A deeply religious man, Milton wrestled with a priestly vocation in the Anglican Church. He judged that it would compromise his religious conscience to join a clergy of a bishop-dominated church. He chose to become a poet and a pamphleteer. One of his strongest polemical efforts is found in his treatise attacking the rule of bishops.

John Calvin (1509–64) organized the Reformed Church in Switzerland, founded the University of Geneva, and created the movement known as Calvinism.

realized that they were not able to live like Englishmen there. So in 1620 they sailed on the *Mayflower* to America and settled in Plymouth, Massachusetts. The Pilgrims aboard the *Mayflower* were Separatists or Congregationalists who had attempted reform of the Anglican Church. They brought Protestantism to America. They were followed later, in 1682, by the Quakers, when William Penn (1644–1718) founded the colony of Pennsylvania.

DEVELOPMENTS IN THEOLOGY

The Lutheran Reform needed to explain its new doctrinal positions that the reformers were establishing. They had to justify why the changes were necessary and indicate the forms they would take and the religious benefits that would flow from the reform teachings. When their teachings were misunderstood they had to clarify the meaning. When their doctrines were attacked the theologians had to defend them. Thus the early reform theologians developed a Protestant scholasticism that competed with the Scholastic theology developed by the Catholic Church. Jacob Schegk (1511–87) is considered the father of Protestant or Lutheran Scholasticism, but its greatest synthesis is found in the writings of Johann Gerhard (1582–1637).

THE CALVINISTS AND THE PIETISTS

Matters were different in Calvinist circles. The theological focal point was biblical. This is evident in the manner in which Calvin spoke, not of the sacrament of the Eucharist, but of the Lord's Supper. The divine covenant with humanity set up a symbol for man's covenant with man: as God related to humanity so humanity should relate to one another. This parallel was developed in *The Economy of the Covenants between God and Man* by Herman Witsius (1636–1708). This theological treatise became the centerpiece for the theology of the American Puritans.

In reaction to the academic character of Protestant Scholasticism, the Pietist movement pushed for a warmer emotional faith. This accent was developed by Nikolaus Zinzendorf (1700–60) and August Hermann Francke (1663–1727) in the 18th and 19th centuries. The Pietist movement also heavily influenced Methodism in the Church of England and eventually led to a schism in 1784 that produced an independent Methodist Church.

THE 19TH AND 20TH CENTURIES

The 19th century marked the beginning of Liberal Protestant theology. Its chief proponent was Friedrich Schleiermacher (1768–1834), whose *On Religion* (1799) appealed to the cultured despisers of Christian dogmas and practices. It discovered religion's basis in "an oceanic feeling" of awe toward the universe, a doctrine that Schleiermacher hoped would appeal to a world filled with romantic optimism.

Karl Barth (1886–1968), at the beginning of the 20th century, reacted against this Liberal theology. He argued that World War I ended the era of humanity's love of itself and humanity's belief that it could create a heaven on earth. His essays on 19th-century evangelical theology and his book *The Humanity of God* were a call for a return to the fundamental Lutheran insights that inspired the original Protestant Reformation.

EFFORTS TO UNITE

The main thrust of Protestantism was in the direction of reform. The result of these continuing reform efforts was the creation and multiplication of new sects. Imitating the conciliatory attempts of Martin Bucer (1491–1551) and John Calvin (1509–64), Charles Brent (1668–1729), an American Episcopal bishop, called for an effort to find ways of having Protestants avoid splintering movements and come together again. This appeal eventually inspired various ecumenical efforts. The Life and Work Movement, which held meetings in Stockholm (1925) and Oxford (1937), attempted to unite the various churches by encouraging them to join a common endeavor in dealing with social and ethical issues. The Faith and Order Movement, which met in Lausanne (1927) and Edinburgh (1937), tried to go beyond a union founded on dealing with practical social and moral issues in an attempt to find a common set of beliefs that could serve as a uniting force. When

The symbol of the World Council of Churches. The word *ecumenical* comes from the Greek work *oikoumene*, meaning "the whole universe."

these movements saw how social, ethical, and doctrinal questions were interrelated, they united to form the World Council of Churches in Amsterdam in 1948. This council still provides a forum for the churches to talk with one another and to provide common initiatives where possible.

CHAPTER 4

BRANCHES OF PROTESTANTISM AND THEIR BASIC BELIEFS

Christianity has undergone many changes over the course of history. The single church of ancient times divided again and again, evolving from one Christian church into many Christian churches, each with its own beliefs and practices. The first division took place when the Nestorians and Monophysites separated from the Christian church in the fifth century. The Nestorians held the belief that in Christ there were two persons, a divine person and a human person. According to them Mary, the mother of Jesus, was only the mother of the human person of Christ; she was not the mother of God. The Nestorians were condemned at the third ecumenical, or general church council, held at Ephesus in 431. The Nestorians of today exist principally in Iraq, with small scattered churches in Syria, Iran, and southern

Canterbury in England has been the seat of the chief archbishop since the time of Saint Augustine in 597 C.E. In 1536, it became the chief cathedral of the newly named Church of England.

India. The Monophysites taught that there was only one nature in Christ, a divine nature. The fourth ecumenical council, held at Chalcedon in 451, condemned this teaching as heresy, or false teaching. Today practicing Monophysites exist in Syria, Egypt, Ethiopia, and Armenia.

THE GREAT SCHISM

The churches that followed the correct teaching of the general church councils, namely, the other Eastern churches and the Western church, were called Orthodox, which is Greek for "correct teaching." However, feuds arose between the East and the West in the ninth century, mostly over authority and appointments. These disputes were revived in 1054, causing the Great Schism. In that year the Orthodox churches separated from the Catholic Church, and attempts over the centuries to heal the division have failed.

Protestantism, a reform movement within the Western or Roman Catholic Church, led to a further split in the Christian church. As indicated earlier, the term Protestant came from the protests by princes and representatives of certain towns in Germany who protested against the emperor's attempt to stop the spread of Lutheranism. These princes and cities came to be known as the "Protesting Estates." The term Protestant thereafter came to include all Christians of continental Europe who left the Catholic Church or were members of a community that descended from a church separated from Rome.

Thus, by the middle of the 16th century, Christianity had divided into three main branches that are still recognized today: Catholicism, Orthodoxy, and Protestantism. Members of the Anglican Church at times refer to themselves as Anglo-Catholics, but in terms of the definition traditionally given, as above, they fall under the classification "Protestantism."

PROTESTANTISM AND ITS BELIEFS

Protestantism, which arose in the Reformation movement of the 16th century, is the youngest branch of Christianity. It actually developed as a series of semi-independent religious movements, each of which rejected the central authority of the pope, rather than as one movement. Cultural, geographic, and political differences caused these movements to develop independently to various degrees. Compared with the unity that characterizes the

In Christian art a dove is often used to symbolize the Holy Spirit.

The Relationship with God

Protestants as a whole share a belief in one God and in the central importance of Jesus Christ as the Savior of humanity. Most denominations also believe in the Trinity of Father, Son, and Holy Spirit. Protestants differ from other Christians about the fundamental relationship between humanity and God. Protestants emphasize the serious effects of original sin on humanity, stressing its moral weakness and inability to do good on its own.

Roman Catholic Church and the Eastern Orthodox Church, which date from the earliest days of the Christian era, Protestantism has itself divided into hundreds of separate denominations and sects. Each of the many denominations has differing beliefs and practices; thus they appear to be entirely distinct from one another. It is difficult, therefore, to discuss Protestantism as a single branch of Christianity.

JUSTIFICATION BY FAITH

The Catholic view of humanity is of a fallen creature. To be restored to dignity as a creature of God, humanity needs the grace of God that lifts it up. When in the state of grace, then, humanity is still prone to sin. Yet God, in the Catholic view, elevates humanity through grace, so that humanity's graced nature is able to perform good works and thus cooperate with God in his salvation. For Protestants this appears to ignore human weakness and to accentuate too strongly humanity's role in redemption.

The consequences of the Catholic position are manifold. By stressing the positive role of humanity's good works in redemption, Catholics tend to focus on externals. The sacraments, for instance, are viewed as acting automatically just by being themselves. There is no focus on the intention of the agents or the motivation of the ministers of the sacraments. Almsgiving likewise tends to be something worthy in itself, with little attention given to the pride that might be the source of this generosity.

Protestants tend to focus on the interior, on the corrupt motives of the almsgiver or the wickedness or unworthiness of the sacramental minister. Protestantism furthermore leans toward the belief that God deals directly with the individual and not necessarily through the instrumentality of the church and its officers.

CENTRALITY OF THE BIBLE

God's direct relationship with the individual is the main reason that translations of the Bible are important according to Protestants. They make the sacred text available to each believer, not only to the learned. All the external trappings of church ceremonies are unimportant for many Protestants. What is central is the word of God in the Bible, speaking directly to people's hearts.

Whereas the beliefs of Catholics are based on both the Bible and church traditions, most Protestants believe that the Bible should be the only authority for their religion. *The Helvetic Confession*, written by Henry Bullinger (1504–75), set out beliefs that are widely used in Reformed churches:

We believe and confess the canonical Scriptures of the holy prophets and apostles of both Testaments to be the true Word of God, and to have sufficient authority of themselves, not of men. For God himself spoke to the

SALVATION BY FAITH IN CHRIST

The idea first put forward by Martin Luther was that salvation is gained by faith in Christ's redemptive death. He said that it is Christ who saves; humanity does not save itself. He said that good works are not abandoned but are expressions of our gratitude for Christ's redeeming death. They play no part, however, in meriting salvation.

Therefore the first care of every Christian ought to be, to lay aside all reliance on works, and strengthen his faith alone more and more, and by it grow in the knowledge, not of works, but of Christ Jesus, who has suffered and risen again for him; as Peter teaches, when he makes no other work to be a Christian one. Thus Christ, when the Jews asked Him what they should do that they might work the works of God, rejected the multitude of works, with which He saw that they were puffed up, and commanded them one thing only, saying: "This is the work of God, that you believe in Him whom He sent, because God the Father has set His seal on Him."

—John 6:29

Christians gathered together for a home
prayer group sharing communion and
reading from the Bible.

fathers, prophets, apostles, and still speaks to us through the Holy Scriptures. And in this Holy Scripture, the universal Church of Christ has the most complete exposition of all that pertains to a saving faith, and also to the framing of a life acceptable to God; and in this respect it is expressly commanded by God that nothing either be added or taken from the same.

Although there are central beliefs shared by most Protestants, there are also many important differences among them. These divergent views have resulted in the division of Protestantism into different religious groups or sects.

THE EARLY PROTESTANT CHURCHES

Even though there are numerous Protestant churches, and it is impossible to describe all the different views of Christian life that they represent, there are the early or root churches that set up many of the basic principles from which the various new religious communities descend.

THE LUTHERANS

Martin Luther (1483–1546), after university studies at Erfurt, Germany, entered a cloister of Augustinian hermits and was ordained a priest in 1507. He received his doctorate in theology at the University of Wittenberg in 1512 and began a teaching career there that lasted all his life. He became deeply involved in the controversy over indulgences, especially in regard to the way that Johann Tetzel (ca. 1465–1519) presented them. For Tetzel indulgences that promised the remission of the temporal punishment due to sin could be obtained by simply giving alms for the restoration of Saint Peter's Basilica in Rome. It seemed to Luther that this was a form of bought forgiveness for oneself

FOUNDERS OF CHRISTIAN CHURCHES

Martin Luther
Lutherans
Menno Simons
Mennonites
Thomas Helwys, John Smyth
Baptists
John Calvin
Presbyterians/Calvinists
John Wesley
Methodists
Joseph Smith
Church of the
Latter-day Saints (Mormons)
Mary Baker Eddy
Christian Scientists
Charles Taze Russell
Jehovah's Witnesses

or a deceased loved one. Luther saw this practice as indicative of the way in which the Catholic Church had strongly compromised the spiritual mission of Christianity and become too worldly in its interests and too external in its portrait of religion.

Mainly through this controversy, Luther arrived at the conclusion that the fundamental differences between the Catholic interpretation and his new interpretation of Christianity were too great. He accentuated the differences in his theology, and these theological positions led to his excommunication by Pope Leo X (r. 1513–21), a condemnation that was carried out in 1521 by Emperor Charles at the Diet of Worms (a lawmaking meeting of princes, nobles, and clergymen).

In his *Babylonian Captivity of the Church*, Luther attacked the mechanical sacramental rituals of the Catholic Church, and in his book *On Christian Liberty* he glorified the freedom of the Gospel that sets believers free from the works required by the Mosaic Law that the Catholic Church imitated. He emphasized the importance of personal faith in contrast to what he considered the slavery of Catholics to a worldly ecclesiastical system.

The chief theologian among Luther's followers was Philip Melanchthon, who drew up the Augsburg Confession that enunciates the basic principles of Lutheran faith. Lutherans retained the Mass but eliminated its significance as an actual sharing in Christ's everlasting sacrifice. For them the Mass was the remembrance of Christ's historical sacrifice. German replaced Latin in the service; and the people were given the right to choose their own pastors. In the worship service the sermon assumed the principal place, for the stimulus of the spoken word was imperative to increase personal faith.

Lutheranism spread to Denmark, Norway, and Sweden, mainly through stu-

Luther's Declaration

When Martin Luther was asked at the Diet of Worms to retract his teachings he declared:

Unless I am convinced by the testimony of the Scriptures or by clear reason (for I do not trust either in the pope or councils alone, since it is well known that they have often erred and contradicted themselves), I am bound by the Scriptures I have quoted and my conscience is captive to the Word of God. I cannot and I will not retract anything, since it is neither safe nor right to go against conscience. I cannot do otherwise.

dents who had studied under Lutheran professors in Germany. It is from these Teutonic nations that Lutheranism spread to North America and other parts of the globe. In the United States many different groups of Lutherans (for example, the American Evangelical Lutheran Church, the Augustana Evangelical Lutheran Church, the Finnish Evangelical Lutheran Church, and the United Lutheran Church in America) formed the Lutheran Church in America in 1962. This group merged with the American Lutheran Church and the Association of Evangelical Lutheran Churches in 1982. So, in effect, in the United States there are two great

In the Augsburg Confession, some of the Catholic feasts were discarded, although Christmas, Easter, and other central festivals were retained. In many parts of Europe it is customary to paint decorations on eggs to celebrate Easter. Eggs symbolize new life.

Lutheran synods or congregations: the ever-merging one we have just described and the Lutheran Church–Missouri Synod, the largest of all the Lutheran groups in the United States. The Missouri Synod, descended from German immigrants who came to the United States in 1847, derives its confession, or expression of beliefs, from the *Book of Concord* (1580).

ULRICH ZWINGLI

For some Luther's reforms did not go far enough. Ulrich Zwingli (1484–1531), a reformer like Luther, also saw abuses in the system of indulgences; but his critique of the Catholic Church was even more radical than that of Luther. He accepted the Bible as the sole authority in religion and his zeal led him to ban processions, festivals, feasts, confessions and penances, and even the organ in church. In brief he was ready to do away with everything the Bible did not explicitly support. In 1529 Zwingli met with Luther in Marburg, Germany, to discuss their differing interpretations of the sacrament of the Eucharist, but they came to no agreement. Luther gave a literal interpretation to Christ's words: "This is My body." For him Christ was really present in the Eucharist. For Zwingli the Eucharist was a sacrament by which we give thanks to God for his gracious gift of the Gospel revelation. The bread and wine are mere symbols of Christ's body and blood. This debate concerning the real or symbolic presence of Christ in the Eucharist caused the first major split in Protestantism.

THE ANABAPTISTS

At the same time, more radical movements emerged in Switzerland and Germany. They rejected infant baptism and instead rebaptised people who were able to make their own profession of faith. They became known as Anabaptists. Their practice was strongly opposed by Luther and Zwingli, and some Anabaptists became revolutionaries in response but were crushed.

In Holland the Anabaptists persisted as Mennonites, taking their name from their leader Menno Simons (1469–1561). The Mennonites follow very closely the Anabaptist tradition.

Mennonites in Pennsylvania harvesting a field using traditional methods. The Mennonites have had strong communities in parts of the United States: For example, in early Germantown, before it became part of Philadelphia; in Lancaster, Pennsylvania; and in many other rural areas of New York, Pennsylvania, and California where their simple life and personal religious commitment could flourish.

The Amish

Under the leadership of Jacob Ammann the Amish communities broke away in the 1690s from the Mennonites. They followed a more strict code of conduct and avoided all other Mennonites. Though originally from Switzerland they now exist only in the United States and Canada, principally in Ohio, Pennsylvania, Indiana, Iowa, and Illinois. They maintain a strict way of life.

They are thus to be distinguished from modern English or American Baptists, whose faith can be traced back to the Puritans who rebelled against the hierarchical structure of the Anglican Church that was ruled by bishops.

THE BAPTISTS

Baptists arose in England in the early 1600s under the leadership of Thomas Helwys (1550–1616) and John Smyth (ca. 1576–1612) but became particularly strong in the 1630s under the Calvinist influence of John Spilsbury (1593–1668). One of the members of his group, Mark Lucar, brought the "new baptism" to New England. The Baptists grew in strength during the 18th century when the Great Awakening, or series of religious revivals that took place in the American colonies in the 1700s, made traveling evangelism popular and pervasive. After the American Revolution, Baptists made impressive advances among the nation. English and American Baptists account for nearly 90 percent of all Baptists worldwide.

THE CALVINISTS

John Calvin (1509–64), although born a Roman Catholic in France, declared himself a Protestant in 1533 and settled in Basel, Switzerland, a year later. There he produced his *Institutes of the Christian Religion* in 1536. This Protestant textbook of theology, written at the age of 26, made him the recognized spokesman for Christian reform in France and Switzerland. In the same year he was asked to become the leader of Geneva's fellowship of Protestant pastors.

Under his leadership the group declared the church superior to the state and demanded the assistance of the state in their attempts to purify church members by strict discipline. This effort earned them banishment at first; but in 1541 the Geneva city council begged Calvin to return and provide able religious and political leadership.

Although he believed that organization could make it easier to enforce purer discipline, he did not wish to imitate the episcopal form of authority characteristic of the Catholic Church, where bishops oversaw all church matters. Rather he wanted the church to be directed by a group of mature lay elders or presbyters, since all lay believers were considered priests. He judged that such an aristocratic body of mature elders was best qualified to enforce religious discipline. Elders were selected based on their qualities of industriousness, self-denial, and thriftiness, characteristics to which all believers should aspire. For Calvin humanity is selfish—in bondage to Satan and saved solely by the grace of God, not its own efforts. Discipline is nonetheless important, since it prevents humanity from falling into bad habits that might undermine its faith in God's grace.

HUGUENOTS AND PURITANS

Calvin's followers were called Huguenots in France and Puritans in England. The Puritans were opposed to Anglicanism because it was episcopal (governed by bishops instead of lay people). In Scotland John Knox (1515–72) came to like Luther's teaching of justification by faith. When Mary Tudor took the throne of England in 1553 and reestablished the Catholic Church as the official Church of England, he fled to Geneva and became Calvin's understudy. When Mary died in 1558 Knox returned to Scotland. Under his leadership the Scottish government made Calvinism or Presbyterianism the state religion in 1560. Until his death in 1572 Knox was the most powerful religious leader in Scotland.

PRESBYTERIAN AND REFORMED CHURCHES

The Calvinist churches are generally called Presbyterian ("ruled by elders") churches in English-speaking countries. Outside of English-speaking countries most churches of this tradition are called Reformed Churches. Reformed, when applied to a church, usually refers to a church that has been reformed according to the biblical Gospel—that is, one that affirms the Bible as the basis of all Christian teaching. The Reformed churches have a tendency, for example, to admit only two sacraments, Baptism and the Lord's Supper, since these they judge to be the only ones explicitly mentioned in the Bible.

Bread and wine are shared during the Lord's Supper, the celebration of Communion.

ANGLICANISM

The development of Anglicanism came in several stages. In 1536, following the 1534 Act of Supremacy by which Henry VIII broke with the Roman Catholic Church, Henry directed that a definition of faith and a book of common prayer be drawn up. With the publication of the "King's Book" in 1546, a creed, or summary of beliefs, was arrived at that was mainly Catholic, except for the emphasis on the authority of the Bible over official church declarations, and on justification by faith rather than by human efforts. During the reign of Henry's daughter Elizabeth I (1558–1603), Parliament drew up another definition of faith and revised the Book of Common Prayer. The articles of faith developed during Elizabeth's reign are still fundamental to the Anglican creed.

The church that evolved under Elizabeth I was a compromise. It took its rules primarily from Martin Luther, but it retained the ritual of the Catholic Church and modeled the church hierarchy on that of the Catholic Church, except that the monarch instead of the pope was considered head of the church. Anglicans today often view themselves as a "bridge church" between Protestantism and Roman Catholicism.

The sacrament of the Holy Eucharist is the central act of worship in the Anglican tradition, as it is in Catholicism and Orthodoxy. The liturgy recalls the story of Christ's sacrifice for the redemption of humankind each time it is offered. Within the Episcopal Church, the Anglican Church in America, Episcopalians differ on how to interpret and practice their faith. Those in the High Church believe in closely following the traditional practices of the church and in the church's authority. The Broad Church, or Liberals, have less strong feelings about tradition. They believe in expressing their faith in various ways, particularly through social action.

The Book of Common Prayer

Anglicans base their religion on scripture, tradition, and reason. They believe in the ancient faith of Christianity as expressed in the Apostles' Creed and the Nicene Creed. The Book of Common Prayer is the collection of liturgy, prayers, and teachings used by the church, and this forms the basis for doctrine and discipline as well as worship. The Book of Common Prayer, the Bible, and a hymnal are the common elements in the various celebrations of the Anglican service.

Low Church, or Evangelicals, emphasize the personal and biblical bases of the faith.

Anglican churches are governed by a hierarchy of bishops, priests, and deacons, as is the Catholic Church. The Archbishop of Canterbury is the spiritual leader of the Anglican Church, and he claims that a line can be traced back through 120 archbishops of the English church to Saint Augustine of Canterbury in 597. The archbishop has, however, no jurisdiction outside his own diocese. Beginning in the 1900s, laypeople have taken an increasingly important role in church affairs.

Every 10 years the Lambeth Conference of bishops meets in London. This conference serves mainly as a consulting and planning body and can only advise the churches it represents.

METHODISM

John Wesley (1703–91), along with his brother Charles, attempted to deepen religious life and fervor within the traditional rituals of the Anglican Church. He formed organized societies that welcomed itinerant, or traveling, preachers, first in London and then throughout the British Isles. These societies were meant to supplement, not replace, the practices of the Church of England.

The Conferences of 1744–47, which brought together representatives from these societies, stressed that salvation comes through good works as well as faith, in the sense that each individual gives proof of the belief that Christ is his or her personal savior by doing good works. These conferences also consolidated the societies that had spread throughout England, Scotland, and Ireland and brought to them a strong family identity. *Minutes of Some Late Conversations between the Revd. Mr. Wesleys and Others*, published in 1749, established Methodism as a new tradition. In 1752 and again in 1755 efforts were made by the Wesleys to persuade the

Constant Reform

From the Lutheran, Baptist, Reformed, and Anglican churches all the other Protestant communities descend. The basic principle of the Reformation was *semper reformanda* (always being reformed). This principle encouraged disagreement, renewal, and continual improvement.

John Wesley preaching in Old Cripplegate Church in London. The itinerant preachers whom John Wesley invited into his societies were so effective in their sermons that the people naturally desired to receive the sacraments from them. This soon led to the transformation of Methodism from a movement meant to supplement the religious life of the Anglican Church to a separate church.

traveling preachers to sign agreements never to leave the communion of the Church of England.

British immigrants brought Methodism to America, and the chief leader was Francis Asbury (1745–1816). He convinced the American Methodists who wanted to separate from John Wesley's English leadership that they should remain in union with him. Paradoxically this preservation of ties with Wesley eventually permitted him to help the Americans to establish the first independent church within Methodism. At the "Christmas Conference" held in Baltimore (1784–85), with Wesley's approval, a new denomination was started, the Methodist Episcopal Church. Only in 1793 did the Wesleyan Methodist Society in England employ the word church, and thus establish itself as a separate entity from the Church of England.

QUAKERISM

The Society of Friends, also known as Quakers, was founded by George Fox (1624–91) in 1647. It received its name from Fox's response to an English judge: "Tremble at the word of the Lord." The judge called Fox a "Quaker" or a "Trembler." Quakers did not accentuate a specific creed, or set of beliefs, but rather stressed inward spiritual experiences. Religiously they were more spontaneous and waited for personal religious experience to provide guidance for their thoughts and actions.

William Penn (1644–1718), America's most famous Quaker, founded his state of Pennsylvania as a commonwealth safeguarding the religious liberties of its communities, especially of the Quaker settlements. The Quakers have no special sacramental life: All life, for them, is sacramental. They are generally against war and militarism.

ORIGINAL AMERICAN PROTESTANT MOVEMENTS

The Protestant churches so far described have had their roots in Europe: Lutherans came from Germany and Sweden, Anabaptists and Mennonites from Switzerland and Holland, Calvinists or Presbyterians from Scotland, and Methodists from England. Yet not all Protestant churches in America are immigrant churches. A number of Protestant churches familiar to Americans originated in the United States. These include the Mormons, Jehovah's Witnesses, and the Pentacostals.

THE CHURCH OF THE LATTER-DAY SAINTS, OR MORMONS

In the last 30 years membership of this church increased by 220 percent to achieve a total of more than 11 million. Of these, almost 6 million are non-Americans. The Mormon Church is rooted in the 1820 visions of God and Jesus Christ claimed by Joseph Smith (1805–44), who organized the movement in Fayette, New York, in 1830. Smith claimed to have found certain golden tablets buried on a hill near Manchester, New York. He translated these hieroglyphic tablets into the Book of Mormon. For Mormons, this book "supports but does not supplant" the Bible.

Opposition to the growing movement forced its members to move to Kirtland, Ohio, and Independence, Missouri, then to Nauvoo, Illinois. Smith himself was murdered in Carthage, Illinois, in 1844. He was succeeded as president by Brigham Young (1801–77). The choice was disputed and the movement split into different sects. The Missouri branch is known as the Latter-day Saints. Young led his followers to Utah's Salt Lake valley, where they arrived in 1847.

The faith of the Mormons is basically that of conservative Protestant churches, with a few exceptions. Their interpretation differs from that of other Christian churches. Taking the names literally, Mormons believe the Father and the Son must have tangible bodies of flesh, while the Spirit alone is spirit. Mormons also believe that people will be punished for their own individual sins, but not for the original sin. People are saved through Christ's death and by obeying the laws and ordinances of the Gospel. Among the latter are faith in Christ, baptism by immersion, repentance, laying on of hands for reception of the Spirit, and observance of the Lord's Supper each Sunday.

Their teaching of polygamy, or marriage with more than one woman, ran into legal difficulties. In 1890 the president of

Salt Lake City Mormon Temple, Utah. The foundational teachings of the Mormon Church are found in the Book of Mormon, along with two other works of Smith: *Book of Doctrine and Covenants* and *Pearl of Great Price*.

the church issued a declaration that officially discontinued the practice of polygamy. Some attribute the phenomenal growth of the Mormon Church in part to its well-organized missionary program, also also to its emphasis on family and wholesome living, and a strict moral code.

THE CHURCH OF CHRIST, SCIENTIST

This church was founded by Mary Baker Eddy (1821–1910) in Boston in 1892. Her inspiration came from an almost instant recovery in 1866 from an injury while reading the story of Christ healing the man sick with palsy (Matthew 9:1–8). For members of this church God is the only power operating on all that is. The tenets of the church are found in Eddy's book *Science and Health with Key to the Scriptures*, along with the Bible, and applied concretely in the world-famous daily newspaper, founded in 1909 by Mrs. Eddy, *The Christian Science Monitor*.

Their teachings say that Jesus is the Teacher or the Shower of the way. Jesus saves people through Truth, Life, and Love as he demonstrated in healing the sick and overcoming sin and death. The founder wrote: "Nothing aside from spiritualization—yea, the highest Christianization—of thought and desire, can give the true perception of God and Christian Science, that results in health, happiness and holiness."

Heaven is described in metaphorical terms. It is not a place, but rather "harmony," "spirituality," and "bliss." Hell, on the other hand, is described as "error," "lust," "remorse," "hatred," "sin," "sickness," "death," and "suffering." In this most spiritualized form of religion, baptism is not a traditional church ceremony but a continuing "purification from all error."

THE JEHOVAH'S WITNESSES

Jehovah's Witnesses were originally called Millennial Dawnists, International Bible Students, and finally Russellites, until they obtained their present name in 1931. The title "Russellites" points to their first president, Charles Taze Russell (1852–1916), who first organized the group in Pittsburgh in 1872. It was incor-

These congregants have centered upon three allies of Satan: 1) the false teachings of the churches; 2) the tyranny of human government; and 3) the oppressions of business. For them the triple alliance of church, government, and commercial powers has destroyed humanity. They thus refuse to salute the flag, to bear arms in war, or to participate in government, because these are expressions of Satan's power over humans.

porated as a congregation, not a church, in 1884, and its headquarters was moved to Brooklyn in 1909.

Just as they refuse the name church, so they refuse to use titles such as Reverend, Rabbi, or Father. Every member is a minister and all preach from the Bible and teach in private homes at least 15 hours each month. The society's message is found in the Bible; in their official journal, *The Watchtower*; and in the many booklets and pamphlets they distribute.

According to the Jehovah's Witnesses, the world originally was under the rule of God. However, Satan took over and since then humankind has followed his rule. They claim that Christ came to the temple of Jehovah in 1918 and inspired Russell's successor as president, Joseph F. Rutherford (1869–1942), to reorganize the movement to fight Satan's legions. He predicted the coming of a major battle, Armageddon. Jehovah's Witnesses believe that Christ is now enlisting the army of the righteous that will completely annihilate the army of Satan. Those who have proved their loyalty to Christ will fill the new earth as Christ takes over his reign. The wicked will not rise again after they are dead.

PENTECOSTALS

The term Pentecostal derives from the description of Pentecost in the Acts of the Apostles: "And they were all filled with the Holy Spirit and began to speak with other tongues, as the Spirit gave them utterance." (Acts 2:4). The chief characteristic of Pentecostals is the emphasis they place on spiritual gifts such as healing and speaking in tongues.

Modern Pentecostalism began in 1901 through the efforts of Charles Fox Parham (1873–1929) in Topeka, Kansas. There, at Bethel College, Parham and Agnes Ozman La Berge (1870–1937) experienced speaking in tongues. The movement grew slowly

until William Joseph Seymour (1870–1922), Parham's student, carried his religious revival to Los Angeles. His Azusa Street mission trained hundreds of evangelists and missionaries who carried the Pentecostal message across America.

Splits in the Pentecostal movement occurred in the 1920s due to class, racial, ethnic, and doctrinal differences. In the late 1920s and in the 1930s, Aimee Semple McPherson (1890–1944) brought new converts and national publicity to Pentecostalism. In the late 1940s and the 1950s Oral Roberts (1918–) and other evangelists created a new enthusiasm for Pentecostalism in the United States and throughout the world. In the late 1950s a neo-Pentecostalism, or Charismatic, movement developed that started to have influence in prayer groups of the more established Protestant churches and among Roman Catholics.

The largest and most important Pentecostal churches are the Church of God, the Pentecostal Holiness Church, the Church of God in Christ, the Assemblies of God, the Pentecostal Assem-

Outside Solid Rock Church in Monroe, Ohio, is the largest statue of Christ in the United States. It is 62 feet (19 meters) high. The church's mission is that through evangelicalism it brings people of all denominations to the saving knowledge of Christ.

blies of the World, the United Pentecostal Church, and the International Church of the Foursquare Gospel.

NEW RELIGIOUS MOVEMENTS

Throughout the second half of the 20th century, a large number of Protestant religious movements developed. Some sociologists might classify these movements as cults, because their founders are living and command absolute obedience and trust in their leader. Those who distrust such movements point to Jim Jones, a Protestant clergyman, who led the People's Temple. In 1978 he ordered his followers, a total of more than 900 individuals, to commit suicide at their commune in Guyana. Such examples can give a bad name to any religious movement that is not "middle of the road." Critics of such labeling remind their opponents that many Protestant churches, such as the Quakers, Mormons, Christian Scientists, Jehovah's Witnesses, and Methodists, were once considered cults.

THE UNIFICATION CHURCH

One of the best-known religious movements that is commonly criticized as a cult is that of the Reverend Sun Myung Moon, a Korean evangelist who established, in 1954, the Holy Spirit Association for the Unification of World Christianity. Popularly this association is called the Unification Church. Its members are often known as the Moonies.

The Reverend Moon claims that he received a vision of Jesus in 1935. In his vision Christ requested that he complete the task of establishing God's kingdom on earth. Christ's work, as Reverend Moon understood the revelation, was incomplete. The Reverend Moon claims to have been called by Christ to be the continuing Messiah, attempting to complete Christ's work of creating God's one kingdom on earth and bringing God's peace to humankind in general.

Within the Unification Church, the Reverend Moon and his wife Hak Ja Han are believed to be—in contrast to Adam and Eve—the True Parents who beget spiritual children with no original sin. Through spiritual weddings dedicated to establishing the spiritual kingdom of God among all Christians—indeed, among all people—the new Messiah will complete the work of Christ. Unification Church weddings, then, have this special meaning and also this special commitment to beget spiritual children who will unify the world.

PROTESTANT WORSHIP AND LITURGY

Although all Protestants worship only one God, various denominations worship him in vastly different ways. Protestant liturgies, or worship services, vary from simple, informal meetings to elaborate ceremonies.

Most Protestant liturgies stress preaching and hearing the Word of God. Protestants believe that God is present in their

SOME PROTESTANT CHURCHES

Adventist	Mennonite
African Methodist Episcopal	Methodist
African Methodist Episcopal Zion	Moravian Church
Amanite	Mormon
Amish	National Baptist Convention
Assemblies of God	Pentecostal Churches
Baptist	Pentecostal Holiness Church
Brethren	Presbyterian
Christian Methodist Episcopal	Progressive National Baptist Convention
Christian Reformed Church	
Christian Scientist	Reformed Church in America
Church of God in Christ	Schwenkfelder
Church of the Nazarene	Seventh-day Adventist
Churches of God	Shaker
Congregationalist	Society of Friends (Quakers)
Disciples of Christ	Swedenborgian
Doukhobor	Unitarian Universalist Association
Hutterite	United Church of Canada
Jehovah's Witness	United Church of Christ
Lutheran	

midst and inspires faith in them when they read, hear, and discuss the Bible. For this reason most Protestant services focus attention on the preacher and the sermon.

The various Protestant denominations disagree about the nature and number of sacraments, but most include at least two in their worship, baptism and communion. Baptism may involve water being poured or sprinkled on the head, or the person may be immersed totally in water. Many denominations practice infant

baptism; in others only individuals who are personally able to affirm their faith in Jesus Christ as their savior are baptized.

Communion, also called the Lord's Supper, is more symbolic in nature for many Protestants than it is for Catholics and Orthodox Christians, who believe that the bread and wine they receive are actually the body and blood of Christ. Where Catholics receive weekly or daily communion, most Protestant churches observe the ritual less often. Some observe it weekly or monthly; others observe it every three months.

CHURCH ORGANIZATION

Most Protestant churches stress the role of church members who are not clergy. Protestantism encourages people to take part in the liturgy through singing and prayer. This serves to establish a sense of community among the members of the congregation. The Society of Friends (Quakers) took this concept to its extreme, dispensing with all forms of clergy. At a Quaker meeting anyone who feels that he or she has received a message from God may speak up.

OBSERVANCES

Some leaders of the Reformation, such as John Calvin, opposed the traditional church calendar of holy days, filled as it was with saints' days, transformed pagan feasts, and the worship of Mary. One of the first Protestant reforms was the abandonment of the veneration of the saints and of Mary, thereby discarding most of the traditional feasts of the Catholic Church.

Many Protestant congregations today, however, do celebrate several of the traditional holy days of Christendom, with special emphasis on the seasons of Advent (the period beginning four Sundays before Christmas) and Lent (which takes place in the last winter months in preparation for Easter). They also celebrate Christmas, Epiphany (January 6, commemorating the manifestation of Christ to the Gentiles in the persons of the Magi), Palm Sunday, Maundy (Holy) Thursday, Good Friday, Easter, and Pentecost Sunday.

CHAPTER 5

RITES OF PASSAGE

Protestants are usually baptized shortly after birth, although some churches wait until the person can freely choose to affirm his or her faith in Christ. When Protestants get married they usually do so in a church ceremony. When seriously ill some receive the sacrament of the anointing of the sick, and a ceremony of burial follows their death. Such ceremonies as baptism, confirmation, marriage, and funerals are, in the language of today's sociologists, rites of passage, because they mark dramatic changes in human existence and acknowledge the passing from one stage of life to another. They are celebrated as special occasions.

The most common rites of passage in and of themselves often have little or nothing to do with religion. For example graduating from high school or college, getting married, and becoming a parent are all rites of passage that do not necessarily have religious significance for all individuals. However many of these benchmarks in life do have religious implications for believers. Marriage, for instance, demands that the couple imitate Christ's

Regardless of how baptism is carried out, the uniting factor is the use of water as a sign and agent of spiritual cleansing.

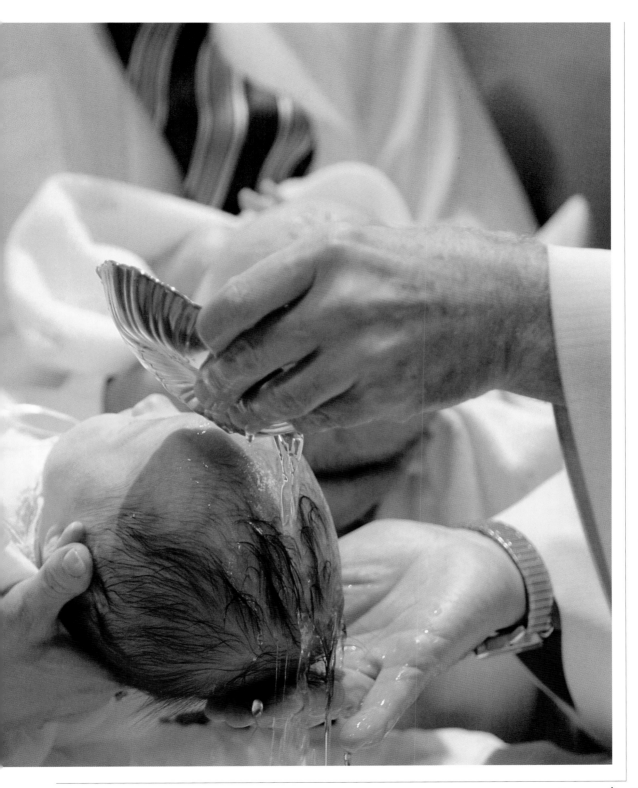

selfless love. Other rites, such as baptism, are strictly religious rites of passage.

SACRAMENTS

In Christian religious ceremonies many of these celebrations of key events are called sacraments—they are signs of divine help or grace needed to live according to the full Christian demands of these stages of life. For instance Christian marriage, as Saint Paul portrays it, commits the husband and wife to try to the best of their ability, with God's help, to live together for the rest of their lives. Their devotion to each other resembles Christ's love for the church—a love that led him to sacrifice his life for his beloved, the members of his church. No human being could live up to this example of Christ without special help or grace from God.

For the Christian, then, marriage is a sign of such a commitment of the spouses to live according to this example of Christ and an acknowledgment that they could not do so without special divine help. A sacrament, furthermore, means that God gives this grace or help with the conferral of the sacrament. For some Protestants elaborate rituals are celebrated at baptism, marriage, and acceptance into holy orders, to signify the new responsibilities and their seriousness and to ask God for the assistance needed to fulfill the demands of these new states of life. For other Protestants there are only the sacraments of baptism and Eucharist, since only those are clearly warranted in the Gospels. The Church of England acknowledges baptism and the Eucharist as sacraments "ordained by Christ" and five others that are "commonly called sacraments" but are "not to be counted for sacraments of the Gospel."

Participants in most rites of passage wear special garments to symbolize the

Rites of Passage

Most rites of passage help a person understand and accept their new role in life. They also serve as a sign to other people that the person should be treated in new ways that are appropriate to their new status. Protestant sacramental rites of passage set up some parallel with Christ's life and show how Christian baptism, confirmation, marriage, or holy orders link Christians to Christ's life and example. They also offer to the Christian the divine assistance to live their life according to this higher ideal.

change they are undergoing. Examples of such dress are graduation caps and gowns, white dresses and veils worn by girls at their First Communion, the clerical robes of ministers, and the wedding gowns and formal attire worn by many brides and grooms.

A discussion of the rites of passage that occur in different Protestant churches at the birth of a child (baptism), during childhood (confirmation), at adulthood (matrimony and holy orders), and at the time of a person's serious illness and death (anointing of the sick) follows.

BAPTISM

The first rite of passage experienced by most Protestants is baptism. For some Protestants baptism occurs within a few days after

BURIED AND RAISED WITH CHRIST THROUGH BAPTISM

The description in Saint Paul's Letter to the Colossians claims a deeper meaning for the rite of passage in Christian baptism:

You were buried with Christ in baptism, in which you also were raised with Him through faith in the working of God, who raised Him from the dead ... Therefore, if you died with Christ from the basic principles of the world, why, as though living in the world, do you subject yourselves to regulations—according to the commandments and doctrines of men? If then you were raised with Christ, seek those things which are above, where Christ is, sitting at the right hand of God. Set your mind on things above, not on things on the earth . . . Therefore, as the elect of God, holy and beloved, put on tender mercies, kindness, humility, meekness, long-suffering; bearing with one another, and forgiving one another . . . Let the word of Christ dwell in you richly in all wisdom, teaching and admonishing one another in psalms and hymns and spiritual songs, singing with grace in your hearts to the Lord.

—Colossians 2:12–3:16

Baptism takes place in many ways in Protestant churches. Baptists practice baptism by total immersion, in the manner of the early Christians, often in rivers and lakes.

birth; for others it is reserved for the period of maturity when a person can make an explicit declaration of faith. Christian baptism marks the entry of an individual into Christian society and association with the Christian faith. The water that is used during the ceremony symbolizes both cleansing from sin and the living, flowing waters of new life in Christ. Baptism is thus the foundation of Christian life, its initiation into the soul of the baptized.

BAPTISM BELIEFS

Various passages in the Bible referring to baptism have led to differences in practice and belief among the various Protestant denominations. Most Protestant churches practice baptism in the name of the Trinity, in accordance with Jesus' instructions to his disciples: "Go therefore and make disciples of all the nations, baptizing them in the name of the Father, and of the Son, and of the Holy Spirit." (Matthew 28:19) Some groups, such as the Baptists, practice baptism after the manner of the early Christians, by total immersion in water. Other groups may baptize by pouring water over the head of the one to be baptized or by sprinkling him or her with water or by the minister's dipping his or her fingers in water and placing them on the candidate's head.

Protestant denominations call baptism a law, and others call it a sacrament. Some groups baptize a person so that he or she may thereby receive the Holy Spirit in accordance with the legal demands of the apostle Peter: "Repent, and let every one of you be baptized in the name of Jesus Christ for the remission of sins, and you shall receive the gift of the Holy Spirit." (Acts 2:38) Others baptize because they believe that the person who is cleansed by water is also cleansed spiritually by God's grace or power. For them, water is a sign, or sacrament, of spiritual cleansing.

GODPARENTS

Some Protestant groups, in particular Anglicans, require godparents, or sponsors, to be present at baptism in addition to the child's parents. The godparents promise to sponsor the child's religious training in case his or her parents for any reason are not able to do so. Most Protestant

The Importance of Baptism

Although some Protestant denominations, such as the Quakers (members of the Society of Friends) and Christian Scientists, do not practice baptism, it is usually viewed by Christians as being necessary for salvation:

He who believes and is baptized will be saved; but he who does not believe will be condemned.

—Mark 16:16

Most assuredly, I say to you, unless one is born again, he cannot see the kingdom of God.

—John 3:5

churches make the parents alone responsible for their child's religious upbringing, and the position of godparent is largely honorary and carries no responsibilities to the child.

UNITY OF BAPTISM

Since Christian baptism is a sign of conversion—that is, of the turning of a person's life toward Jesus Christ—the baptism of adults throughout Christian history has been preceded by a long period of introduction to the faith. Before the baptism of a child in certain Protestant churches, a baptismal conversation takes place with the parents and godparents, who will later introduce the child to the faith. The parents and godparents, answering for the child, must renounce Satan, the evil one, and confess their faith in God, the almighty Father, in Jesus Christ, the Son of God, and in the Holy Spirit.

Christians believe that by being united with Christ through baptism they are also united with all other Christians. Through baptism a community is created that goes beyond all natural boundaries of nations, cultures, races and creeds, tribes, social classes, and sex.

CHRISTENING

Christening, or naming an infant, often takes place formally at the time of baptism. The custom of bestowing a name on the newly baptized child dates from early Christian times, when a person took a new name at baptism. The new name was the name of a saint who was to serve as a model and inspiration during life for the person baptized.

Some Protestant denominations, such as the Anabaptists and Baptists, reject the practice of infant baptism. Their belief is that a person cannot enter the church until he or she is old enough to declare his or her own acceptance of faith in Jesus Christ. Baptists in particular view this rite of passage as giving people participation in the mission of Jesus: Through baptism every believer in effect becomes a priest, required to bear witness to Jesus.

CONFIRMATION

Another rite of passage that takes place at different ages for members of some Protestant churches is confirmation. As a rite of passage confirmation signals the movement of a Christian into fuller membership in the church. Confirmation is thus a symbol of Christian maturity. Preparation of a child for confirmation in some Protestant churches is viewed as the task of the entire community, but in particular of the child's parents and godparents. Children who are to be confirmed study their faith in small groups. In certain churches common experiences and community tasks of dedicated service also accompany and support the lessons learned through the catechism.

In the Church of England the bishop, the traditional celebrant of confirmation, places his hand on the head of the child being confirmed and signs the child's forehead in the form of a cross with chrism, or holy oil. Oil is a symbol of strength, and this anointing is a sign that God will provide those being confirmed with the strength they will need to face the trials of faith that might come to them through life.

MARRIAGE

As a rite of passage marriage moves a man and woman from the unmarried state to the state of being together. Christian marriage is compared with the sacred union of Christ and his church. Through the sacrament or ceremony of matrimony, the couple is called to imitate Christ's love for his people, the church, especially as a sign of the sacrificial form of love that Christ showed in his freely chosen suffering and death for humankind.

Protestants often prepare for marriage by receiving pastoral counseling. It is the duty of the pastor to ensure that the couple is aware of the civil and Christian responsibilities they will face as a married couple and as parents.

MARRIAGE VOWS

At the altar, the bride and groom exchange marriage vows and accept each other as husband and wife. The groom puts a wedding ring on the ring finger of the bride's left hand (in some countries, the traditional wedding ring finger is on the right hand), and the bride may also give the groom a ring. After the ceremony the bride and groom kiss and make their way out of the church down the main aisle, followed by the rest of the wedding party.

Placing the ring on the third finger of the left hand seals the completion of the marriage vows in many Christian countries. In places in which the ring is placed on a finger of the right hand, the significance is still the same.

In the traditional religious ceremony the bridesmaids and ushers walk slowly down the center aisle of the church to the altar. They stand on either side of the altar throughout the ceremony, the ushers at the groom's side and the bridesmaids at the bride's side. The groom enters through a side door and waits for the bride at the altar. The bride then walks down the aisle with her father or father and mother. The bride usually wears a white dress and veil, and she carries a bouquet. When they reach the altar the father (or the father and the mother), according to ceremonial rule, entrusts the bride to the groom.

Infinite variations exist on the traditional ceremony. Music is often played during the procession and recession. Sometimes the couple may write their own wedding service. Songs, poetry, and readings from the Bible may be part of the service. Attendants may include flower girls and ring bearers as well as bridesmaids and ushers. The bride may walk down the aisle unaccompanied, or accompanied by both of her parents, or the bride and groom may enter together. In contrast to the elaborate and ceremonial nuptial Mass of an Anglican couple is the simple wedding of members of the Society of Friends (Quakers), who have no clergy. Quakers marry at a public gathering where they declare their commitment to each other.

A wedding is usually followed by the sharing of food and drink with guests, once again a sign that marriage itself will demand on the part of the couple a life of generosity toward one another and to others. The celebration can be a simple buffet in the church hall or a lavish party with a band and a full-course dinner.

ORDINATION OR HOLY ORDERS

During his lifetime Jesus selected disciples to help him carry out his mission to spread the gospel. The Twelve Apostles were not his only disciples. At one time he sent out 70. After his resurrection, Christian doctrine teaches, Jesus confirmed his disciples' special calling and mission to preach, baptize, and forgive sins. From the earliest beginnings of the Christian church certain men and women have felt a special calling to serve God.

Preparation for a life of dedicated service in a church of any denomination involves years of study in a theological seminary, which is a school for training members of the clergy. In addition to academic subjects, seminary students usually take comprehensive classes in the doctrines, sacred writings, history, and philosophy of their church. They may also study practical subjects, such as pastoral psychology and counseling.

The ceremonies associated with ordination into the clergy vary according to the religious denomination. The man or woman ordained is enabled to act "in the person of Christ." His or her task is to preach and teach, to confer the sacraments, and to lead the people who are entrusted to him or her. Men and women sometimes also dedicate themselves to a life of service within the church as lay ministers.

SICKNESS AND DEATH

Belief in the resurrection of Christ and that through faith in Christ humankind can be resurrected to eternal life is at the heart of Christian belief. When death is seen as a passage to eternal life, it can be accepted and even welcomed.

Christian tradition calls death "the end of a person's pilgrim state" or "the end of a person's life as a wayfarer." All one's life, in a sense, is viewed as a preparation for death. Death is the end of a person's responsibility for shaping his or her earthly life and working to achieve salvation through the grace of God. This life is a prologue to another life. Death, then, for the Christian is not an end but is an entry into a higher form of life.

ANOINTING OF THE SICK

Although the Anglican sacrament of anointing of the sick is not limited to people who are dying, it plays a role in the preparation of a person for death. The sacrament is administered by a priest, who anoints the sense organs of the seriously sick or dying person with consecrated oil and says, "Through this holy anointing may the Lord in his love and mercy help you with the grace of the Holy Spirit. Amen. May the Lord who frees you from sin save you and raise you up. Amen."

DEATH

The final part of the rite of passage that is death is the funeral. Although funeral customs may vary, many of the same practices are carried out throughout the Protestant world: public announcement of the death, preparation of the body, funeral services, a procession, burial or cremation (burning of the body), and mourning.

Preparation of the body usually consists of laying out and washing the corpse and sometimes anointing it with oils. In

THE SECOND COMING OF CHRIST

According to Christian belief, at the end of the world Christ will come again, and the souls of all people will be reunited with their bodies. Then, according to the Bible:

The Son of man will send out His angels, and they will gather out of His kingdom all things that offend, and those who practice lawlessness, and will cast them into the furnace of fire. There will be wailing and gnashing of teeth. Then the righteous will shine forth as the sun in the kingdom of their Father.

—Matthew 13:41–43

The Creed

The last statement of the Apostles' Creed, the traditional affirmation of the Christian faith, reads:

I believe in the Holy Spirit; the holy Catholic Church; the Communion of Saints; the Forgiveness of sins; the resurrection of the body; and Life everlasting.

the United States and in many countries in Europe, where burial may be delayed for several days, most bodies are preserved by a special process called embalming to retard decay. If the body is to be viewed by mourners, makeup will be applied to give the corpse a more lifelike appearance. The body is then dressed in new clothes or wrapped in a cloth called a shroud and placed in a coffin, or casket.

During the period between death and burial relatives and friends come to view the body, if it is displayed, and to express their sympathies to the family. In some countries a wake, or a watch, may be held. Traditionally the wake allows the mourners to pray for the dead and to console the living in their loss.

Funeral services vary widely and may include prayers and hymns or other music. They also include speeches called eulogies, in which those who knew the dead person will often recall

A family grieving at a funeral. A funeral fills important emotional needs for the family and friends of the dead person. It focuses attention on their grief and provides a public ceremony that helps them acknowledge and accept their loss. It also gives them an opportunity to express their feelings and discharge their grief.

incidents from the person's life and praise the person for his or her good nature or accomplishments. After the service a procession of cars usually follows the hearse carrying the corpse to a cemetery. A final brief ceremony is held at the grave before the body is buried or cremated. After the funeral the mourners often return with the family of the dead person to their home or to another place and share food and consolation.

CHAPTER 6

THE IMPACT OF PROTESTANTISM

Protestantism, throughout its history, has had a profound impact on every aspect of human life in the lands where it has been practiced. Nowhere is this more evident than in the United States, where it has played a significant role in shaping the American dream of an ideal society. In 1620 the Pilgrims brought their version of Protestantism to America and gradually established communities throughout the 13 colonies. As America spread west, these Protestants took their beliefs with them and established new religious communities in the midwest and later along the West coast. Hymns such as "America, the Beautiful," written by Katharine Lee Bates (1859–1929), have inspired Americans for more than a century to chase the dream of a united society: "America, America, God shed his grace on thee, and crown thy good with brotherhood from sea to shining sea." This inspiring work was written by the child of a Protestant clergyman.

The Salvation Army was founded by William Booth (1829–1912) to help the poverty-stricken in London, England, in the 1860s under the name of the Christian Mission. In 1878 the name was changed to the Salvation Army.

MOVEMENTS FOR SOCIAL CHANGE

The antislavery movement in the United States had many Protestants among its leaders. *Uncle Tom's Cabin*, the book that fanned the movement to fever heat, was written by Harriet Beecher Stowe (1811–96), the daughter and wife of Protestant clergymen. After the Emancipation Proclamation (1863) Protestants from the North, through their churches and societies, devoted much effort to creating higher education opportunities for those who were freed. When they were able, black Protestants built many schools and colleges.

TEMPERANCE

The temperance movement, which attempted to limit the excessive use of alcohol, was initiated by Protestant clergymen at the beginning of the 19th century. This league of prohibitionists was a major force in the passing of the Eighteenth Amendment, which curtailed "the manufacture, sale, or transportation of intoxicating liquors within, the importation thereof into, or the exportation thereof from the United States and all territories subject to the jurisdiction thereof for beverage purposes."

PEACE

The movement for world peace arose from the different peace societies founded by Protestants that came to form the American Peace Society in 1828. With war on the horizon the Church Union was formed in 1914, and it organized the World Alliance for International Friendship through churches to push for peace at an international level. The League of Nations was chiefly established through the efforts of Woodrow Wilson (1856–1924) the son and grandson of Presbyterian clergymen and a deeply dedicated Presbyterian layman himself. John Foster

Social Gospel

The so-called Social Gospel, accentuating Christ's dedication to the poor and the sick, was prominent in Protestant circles in the later decades of the 19th century and continued on through the 20th century. It sought to eliminate poverty, to curtail the exploitation of the poor by the rich, to reduce the threat of war, to root out corruption in public and private life, and to usher in the kingdom of God.

Dr. Albert Schweitzer (1846–1956) was winner of the Nobel Peace Prize. He was recognized for his humanitarian efforts at the hospital he built in Lambaréné in present-day Gabon.

Dulles (1888–1959), another Presbyterian layman and the son of a Presbyterian clergyman, was the chief American creator of the United Nations.

Despite, then, the constitutional separation of church and state in the United States many of the laws and ethical expectations of our society reflect Protestant origins, derived substantially from the European countries that gave it birth and enjoyed the first fruits of its inspiration. What follows is a concise survey of the influence of Protestantism on education, art, architecture, music, and literature in the United States and around the world.

EDUCATION

Christ's first apostles were not scholars. They were fishermen. Christ did not think that scholars were in any special way qualified to preach the gospel. Some early Christians, like Tertullian in the early third century, preferred a Christianity that was characterized by the simplicity of the fisherman rather than by the intellectual investigation of the scholar. To Tertullian and some other Christians the wisdom of this world seemed to undermine the teachings of the gospel. For example the schools of the classical world of Greece and Rome used for their basic texts the works of writers such as Homer and Virgil, with their tales of vengeful and sensual pagan gods and stories of heroes who seemed to lack many Christian virtues, especially the virtue of humility.

Protestants could have easily heeded the voice of early Christian writers like Tertullian. Learning could lead to pride, and also to corruption of the mind and heart, if the wrong texts were studied. Yet the importance of education to help preach and explain the Protestant vision of life, and to defend it against misinterpretation and direct attacks, required able and well-organized training. During the Reformation of the 1500s Protestant sections of Europe began to establish elementary schools to teach the children of common citizens to read the Bible in their native languages. Most Protestant colonists who came to America from Europe set up the kinds of schools they had known in their homelands. The teaching of reading was fostered in colonial New England in

Protestants put emphasis on the Bible as the focus for worship and study so that congregations are gathered around the Scriptures.

the belief that by knowing the Scriptures people would be able to defeat the power of the devil.

Protestants established and supported their own schools. Most of these were elementary schools where reading, writing, and religion were taught. Later secondary schools and even small

Borgund stave church. Wooden stave churches date from medieval times and are unique to Norway.

colleges were founded by Protestant churches, primarily to train young men for the ministry. Many of these colleges developed in the 20th century into large and respected universities. Harvard, Yale, Boston University, Duke, Southern Methodist, Emory, and Brigham Young all have Protestant origins.

ARCHITECTURE AND ART

Although the Christian church did not continue many of the ritual laws of the Jewish people, they did cling to the Ten Commandments. The first commandment prohibits the making of images of anything in heaven or on earth that could serve as an idol. This prohibition made the early Christians hesitate to create any images. Some Protestant traditions opposed images of every kind and at all times and places. The Catholic crucifix with the body of Christ was replaced by a bare wooden cross. Sometimes even the cross was prohibited.

CHRISTIAN BUILDINGS

Architects in the early part of the Middle Ages were creative. They constructed churches that were based on a style of building that had been developed in the era of Rome's greatness. A more definitively Christian form of architecture was adopted later in the Middle Ages with the development of majestic Gothic cathedrals, such as Chartres in France, with arches and towers that seemed to soar to heaven. These cathedrals were intended to inspire a mood of reverence among worshippers, lifting their hearts to the heavens above. The Gothic style was developed to enhance the mystery and remoteness of the transcendent drama of the Mass. The Mass was a reenactment of the eternal sacrifice Christ offers to his Father. For Protestants in later centuries, however, such buildings were too majestic, too distracting from the centerpiece of their religion, the Bible.

Protestant Architecture

More recently, in the era of a more ecumenical Protestantism, Protestant architecture has become more creative. This can be seen in the churches designed by Frank Lloyd Wright (1867–1959), Ludwig Mies van der Rohe (1886–1969), Eero Saarinen (1910–61), and Rudolf Schwartz (1859–1935).

The interior of U.S. architect Frank Lloyd Wright's Unity Temple in Oak Park, Illinois, which has a cubic design. The building is a National Historic Landmark.

The churches of the first Protestants were, like the cathedral of Ulm in Germany, former Catholic churches. At times they did not build new churches but took over former Catholic ones. Their general tendency was just to simplify them. They removed the distracting stained-glass windows and the rood screen that fostered a sense of mystery at the expense of communication and communion among the gathered people. They removed the statues, centered the Bible on the altar, encircled the altar and pulpit with pews that faced one another, and created a congregation gathered around the Scriptures. Often the walls were painted white to enable the congregation to concentrate their attention on the Bible. The first Protestant churches looked like Catholic churches, but simpler and less adorned.

When Protestants built their own churches they often tended to be like New England congregational meetinghouses. They were wooden, white, with plain glass. The accent in these buildings is on the pulpit and alignment of the pews rather than on the baptismal font and the altar. Christopher Wren (1632–1723), who was the architect for Saint Paul's Cathedral in London, built most of his churches according to the Protestant ideal: They are settings for intimacy, for seeing and hearing.

CHRISTIAN ART

The Reformation brought lean days for art in northern Europe. Under the influence of the developing Protestant churches the demand for religious art lessened and visual art in general came under suspicion as leading to idolatry, the religious worship of idols. The Lutheran Church ignored art; the Calvinist Church condemned it. Only in the Netherlands did art survive the Reformation. Lucas Cranach (1472–1553) has left us a portrait of Luther; and Albrecht Dürer (1471–1528), known as the "first Protestant artist," describes Luther as "that Christian man who helped me out of great anxieties." Dürer painted *The Four Apostles* in 1523 and shows the apostle John holding a Bible opened to a text revealing Luther's 1521 German translation of the text.

It is to the Netherlands that we must turn if we wish to find any significant contributions from Protestant artists. Rembrandt (1606–69) can be considered a Protestant artist for a number of reasons: He rejected the pagan themes of the Italian Renaissance that ruled much of the art of his era, he avoided all excesses and theatrics, and he found drama in the commonplace settings of life. He thus brings out the simple humanity of Christ who is seen in humble settings, and whose only crown is a crown of thorns.

The lasting influence of the Reformation on the art world was that it pushed the production of art more into the secular arena. Whereas the medieval artist's patron had been the church, the artist of the Reformation and thereafter was sponsored by monarchs, princes, and the wealthy. Scenes from daily life replaced religious scenes as the primary focus of painting, while architects turned their talents to the design of palaces and great houses rather than cathedrals. From their former status as anonymous

The Feast of the Rose Gardens by Albrecht Dürer (1471–1528), who is known as "the first Protestant artist."

servants of the church, artists became professionals who proudly signed the pictures they painted.

MUSIC

Christianity played an important part in the early growth of classical music, manifested especially in the harmonic genius of Franz Joseph Haydn (1732–1809), Wolfgang Amadeus Mozart (1756–91), and Ludwig van Beethoven (1770–1827). However this was not the first influence Christianity had on music.

PLAINSONG AND HYMNS

The oldest known Christian form of music was plainsong, a simple form of vocal music that was used in early Christian church services. Plainsong was so called because a soloist or choir sang the melody without instrumental accompaniment or harmony. Plainsong developed gradually from early Jewish religious music and much of it was set to the words of the Psalms.

Some of the most appreciated Protestant hymns share in this simple tradition. The Geneva Psalter, inspired by John Calvin, has preserved an uncompromising and uncorrupted simplicity in its vocal and vernacular expression of faith. This has influenced the music of the Reformation in England, where psalms were set to simple chant. It has to be noted that Martin Luther himself endorsed the use of music in worship. He played the lute and wrote notable hymns. "A Mighty Fortress Is Our God," a free rendering of Psalm 46, became known as the battle hymn of the Reformation. Here is the message of one of his Easter hymns:

It was a strange and dreadful strife
When life and death contended;
The victory remained with Life,
The reign of death was ended;
Stripped of power, no more he reigns,
An empty form alone remains,
His sting is lost forever!
Alleluia!

CHORALE AND ORATORIO

Many different forms of classical music were created for church services. The German Reformation gave rise to a particular type of hymn called the chorale. This achieved its high point under Johann Sebastian Bach (1685–1750), who took over this basic form and used it as the foundation of his great masses and cantatas. In his era we witness not only the elevation of choral music and the writing of melodious chorales, but also the birth of the organ as a key instruement.

Another form of music that developed under the influence of Protestant musicians is the oratorio, a musical composition that uses soloists, chorus, and orchestra. The subject is usually taken from the Bible, and the first and most popular subject was the Passion, or sufferings, of Christ. Perhaps the most famous is Bach's *Passion According to Saint Matthew*. George Frideric Handel (1685–1759) was the greatest writer of oratorios, of which he composed 15. The best known is *The Messiah*, the singing of which has become a Christmas tradition worldwide.

PROTESTANT SIMPLICITY IN HYMNS

This poem, often now sung as a hymn, comes from Saint Paul's Letter to the Colossians:

Praise to the Lord, the Almighty, the King of creation!
O my soul praise him, for he is thy health and salvation!
All ye who hear, now to his temple draw near;
Praise him in glad adoration.
Praise to the Lord! Who o'er all things so wondrously reigneth,
Shelters thee under his wings, yea, so gently sustaineth;
Hast thou not seen how thy desires e'er have been
Granted in what he ordaineth?
Praise to the Lord! O let all that is in me adore him!
All that hath life and breath, come now with praises before him!
Let the Amen sound from his people again;
Gladly for aye we adore him.

—Colossians 2:12–3:16

PROTESTANT INFLUENCES ON MODERN MUSIC

The influence of the Protestant tradition on music has extended into the late 20th century. Major works have been inspired by religious motifs, such as Benjamin Britten's (1913–76) *War Requiem*, and Gian Carlo Menotti's (1911–2007) opera *Amahl and the Night Visitors*. The musicals *Joseph and the Amazing Technicolor Dreamcoat*, *Godspell*, and *Jesus Christ Superstar* were successful attempts to retell scriptural stories in a contemporary musical style. These theatrical productions, aimed primarily at young people, who might be more comfortable with contemporary music than with the more traditional oratorio form, were huge box-office hits.

LITERATURE

At the beginning of the Reformation theological writings were the main focus of literary activity. Reform writers delved primarily into the meaning of the Bible and wrote treatises and commentaries in which they gave their interpretations of the biblical texts. They strongly criticized nonbiblical works as products of self-centered men. However, two great works of imagination produced in the Reformed tradition stand out both for their literary worth and as examples of Christian faith. These are John Milton's (1608–74) *Paradise Lost* and John Bunyan's (1628–88) *Pilgrim's Progress*. Of *Paradise Lost* Andrew Marvell (1621–78) wrote:

The majesty which through thy work doth reign
Draws the devout, deterring the profane
And things divine thou treat'st of in such state
As them preserves, and thee, inviolate.

George Frideric Handel's Biblical Oratorios

Esther

Belshazzar

Deborah

Judas Maccabaeus

Saul

Joshua

Israel in Egypt

Alexander Balus

Messiah

Susanna

Samson

Solomon

Joseph and His Brethren
Jephtha

For the Resurrection of Our Savior Jesus

For Jesus, Suffering and Dying for the Sins of the World

This is a wonderful tribute to Protestantism's greatest writer. The judgment is based on a Protestant measure: Milton had not gotten in the way of the fundamental biblical story.

In the United States Nathaniel Hawthorne (1804–64) and Herman Melville (1819–91) continued the Protestant tradition, despite their difficulties with their churches over the complexities of morality, sin, and redemption. They worked within the inherited motifs of good and evil that filled the hearts and minds of New England Puritans but focused also on the importance of brotherhood and sins of intellectual pride.

PROTESTANTISM AND THE THEATER

Christianity's influence on the theater was at first negative. In Rome many forms of theater were popular—tragedy, comedy, farce, and pantomime. Most of these performances were offensive to the early Christians, however, and as Christianity grew more powerful the Roman theater declined. In the 400s, actors were excommunicated from the church, and Roman theater came to an end not long afterward. The last known theatrical performance in ancient Rome was in 533.

FROM THE MIDDLE AGES THROUGH THE REFORMATION

During the late Middle Ages European townspeople and villagers often staged Passion plays, plays that depict the suffering, crucifixion, and death of Jesus Christ. They also developed morality plays, miracle plays, and mystery plays, which were tied very much to religious belief and practice. By the time of the Reformation, the connection between church and theater had disappeared. Instead of aiding the church's worship, the theater became more of a competitor. This reached a peak in London around 1600, where the plays of William Shakespeare had more influence over the masses than religious preachers. In Protestant eyes, the new dramas were more to be condemned than to be supported.

The Reformation, however, also had a positive effect on the history of drama. The positive effect was its promotion of the vernacular over the use of Latin. The use of local languages

TRANSLATIONS OF THE BIBLE

Two of the greatest Protestant literary achievements were translations. Luther's translation of the Bible into German provided a benchmark as both a literary and a religious work. The same can be said of the King James translation of the Bible into English. They are magnificent achievements of literature. The King James version of John's Gospel opens with the words:

In the beginning was the Word, and the Word was with God, and the Word was God.
The same was in the beginning with God.
All things were made by him; and without him was not any thing made that was made.
In him was life; and the life was the light of men.
And the light shineth in the darkness; and the darkness comprehended it not.
There was a man sent from God, whose name was John.
This same came for a witness, to bear witness of the Light, that all men through him might believe.
He was not that Light, but was sent to bear witness of that Light.
That was the true Light, which lighteth every man that cometh into the world.
He was in the world, and the world was made by him, and the world knew him not.
He came unto his own, and his own received him not.
But as many as received him, to them gave he power to become the sons of God, even to them that believe on his name:
Which were born, not of blood, nor of the will of the flesh, nor of the will of man, but of God.
And the Word was made flesh, and dwelt among us, and we beheld his glory, the glory as of the only begotten of the Father, full of grace and truth.

—John 1:1-14

eventually led to the development of national drama in many countries. Theater flourished in England and France. England, however, experienced the negative effect of the Reformation when the Puritans gained control of Parliament in the 1640s and prohibited theatrical performances. The Puritan government closed the English theaters in 1642. They remained closed until the restoration of King Charles II (1630–85) in 1660. Puritan disapproval of theatrical performances also affected theater in the United States.

THEATER TRANSCENDING RELIGION

The general Protestant opposition to the theater has long since disappeared. Individual plays might still draw religious objections due to what some consider their antireligious or immoral content. The theater today, however, has become much more an instrument of distraction and enjoyment, so many plays are aimed to please audiences of different religions or none at all. More serious plays often have a generally acceptable moral lesson as they attempt to bring about needed social changes, to overcome prejudices, or to make people appreciate the common humanity they share with others. Even religious plays such as John Osborne's Luther are able to focus on the intensity of a religious person's life in a way that transcends the person's historical links. The success of William Butler Yeats's Abbey Theatre in Catholic Dub-

T. S. (THOMAS STEARNS) ELIOT

T. S. (Thomas Stearns) Eliot (1888–1965) ranks among the most important poets of the 20th century. He was an "Anglo-Catholic in religion" who criticized in his poems and dramas the spiritual bankruptcy of Europe. *Ash Wednesday* (1930), Four Quartets (1936–42), and his play *Murder in the Cathedral* (1935) are deeply religious and provide a profound meditation on time and eternity, as does this excerpt from *The Rock* (1934):

The Rock

The endless cycle of idea and action,
Endless invention, endless experiment,
Brings knowledge of motion, but not of stillness;
Knowledge of speech, but not of silence;
Knowledge of words, and ignorance of the Word.
All our knowledge brings us near to our ignorance,
All our ignorance brings us nearer to death,
But nearness to death no nearer to God.
Where is the Life we have lost in living?
Where is the wisdom we have lost in knowledge?
Where is the knowledge we have lost in information?

T.S. Eliot, one of the 20th century's greatest poets in the English language, explored Christian themes in many of his works

lin—which staged many plays by Protestant playwrights such as Oscar Wilde, George Bernard Shaw, John Millington Synge, Sean O'Casey, Samuel Beckett, and Yeats himself—shows the changed religious atmosphere regarding the theater.

Today one can find drama or theater programs run at Protestant churches, such as the Trinity House Theatre in Livonia, Michigan, or at universities with Protestant affiliations, such as Duke and Yale.

CHAPTER 7

PROTESTANTISM FACING NEW CHALLENGES

Contemporary challenges to Christianity have often come about through the secularization and modernization of society. The increasing worldliness of society has at times caused a decline both in the numbers of some Christian denominations and in the social and political influence of these churches. The secularization of the modern world has also put pressures on the churches to change many of their attitudes. Some have adapted in order to meet these demands and preserve their relevance; others continue to resist, viewing these demands as the fleeting pressures of our times.

PROTESTANTISM IN A SECULAR WORLD

In earlier centuries the Protestant churches of western Europe and America influenced every aspect of life: family life, work, education, art, and politics. In the 20th century the sphere of the church's influence has often been narrowed to its effect on individuals and family life. To continue to carry out their mission to

More than 4,000 envoys from 350 churches around the world participate in an outdoor meeting during the Ninth Assembly by the World Council of Churches in Porto Alegre, Brazil, on Tuesday, February 21, 2006.

the poor, the hungry, and the sick, and to spread the gospel of love, Protestant churches have had to revitalize their congregations through many new movements.

ECUMENISM

One effort to overcome the continual splintering within Protestantism and to promote common Christian efforts has been the ecumenical, or unification, movement. This movement began in the early decades of the 20th century and for many years was almost exclusively confined to Protestantism. At the international level the World Council of Churches was formed in Amsterdam, the Netherlands, in 1948. The council brings together almost all the Christian churches, except for the Catholic Church. It works to promote cooperation and unity among all the churches of the world and has opened discussions with non-Christian groups such as Buddhists and Muslims as well.

Among the council's united activities are education, missionary work, aid to refugees, and the promotion of world peace. It has studied the role Christians should play in improving government and various social institutions, and it has sponsored studies on the future of society in an age of rapid scientific and technological progress.

On the national level many Protestant groups have combined and formed new denominations. For example, in the United States the United Church of Christ brought together Evangelical, Reformed, and Congregational churches. In Canada Methodists, Congregationalists, and Presbyterians formed the United Church of Canada. The National Council of Churches in the United States brings many Protestant and Orthodox groups together to coordinate various activities.

The goal of ecumenism is for churches to turn their energies away from defending their denominational boundaries and to begin coming together in prayer and worship as well as in other church activities. The possibility of a reunion between the Catholic and Protestant churches has become more realistic within each tradition. However, although Catholics and Protestants can cooperate in prayer and work, agreement about the basic tenets of the faith—such as the affirmation of the divine and human natures in Christ, an appreciation of the church as the mystical body of Christ, and a deeper understanding of the church's sacraments—must come before there can be any full union. The ecumenical movement, however, has given Christians from many denominations common grounds for developing cooperative energies in today's world.

CHARISMATIC CHRISTIANITY

Another response to the challenges of a more secular society came in a movement called charismatic Christianity, which stresses personal experience of the Holy Spirit apart from sacraments and church institutions. The movement began with the founding of Pentecostalism in the United States in 1901. Pentecostalism takes its name from the feast of Pentecost, when the apostles experienced the outpouring of the Holy Spirit. Charismatic groups usually meet in houses rather than churches, although prayer meetings may also be held in a church. The meetings are energetic and emotional and include periods of singing, silent meditation, and spontaneous prayer and testimony. There is little if any clerical leadership at charismatic meetings, making the participation of the individual more immediate and vital. In the 1960s the Jesus Movement, a form of charismatic Christianity that now calls itself the Jesus People Movement, became popular among young people. It combined elements of Pentecostalism with features of the way of life of the young, such as the use of rock music in hymns.

THE FOUNDING OF NEW RELIGIOUS DENOMINATIONS

In Europe the founding of a new church generally was a conscious act of dissent against the established church of the country. In the United States, which guaranteed freedom of religion and had no established church or orthodox tradition, a new church was the natural outcome of almost any new idea. In 19th-century New York the law stated that six persons could constitute a religious society, or church. Consequently Protestantism has historically divided itself into new groups whenever disagreements arose. Even though this process has often made the two groups weaker, it has at times served to foster renewal that has released new energies. One instance was the establishment of the Progressive National Baptist Convention by Martin Luther King Jr. in his split from the National Baptist Convention.

Another attempt to revive the spirit of Christianity was the "born-again" movement, in which believers reaffirmed their faith in Jesus through their experience of being born again into a new and more committed life as Christians. At the core of these charismatic movements has been an attempt to involve the individual in a more immediate and vital way, to make religion more personal and direct. It has tapped new energies by reawakening a more personal faith and by filling a vacuum in societies that have become more and more impersonal and distant.

Members of Temple of Deliverance Church of God and Christ, led by Bishop G.E. Patterson.

PRIESTHOOD AND MINISTRY

In many Protestant churches a shortage of ministers has raised concern. In others the limiting of ministry or priesthood to men has raised cries of inequality. Traditionally women have been excluded from the Anglican priesthood, a condition that existed until recently despite challenges that began with the women's suffrage movement at the turn of the 19th century. In 1853 Antoinette Brown (1825–1921) became the first woman minister to be ordained in America. She served a Congregational church in New York State. However, it was a long time before women became ordained in any numbers. The lead in ordination of women was taken by the Lutheran Church in Denmark, which ordained three women ministers in 1948. Today women ministers serve in almost all Protestant denominations.

ORDINATION OF WOMEN PRIESTS WORLDWIDE

The ordination of 11 women to the Episcopalian priesthood in the United States in 1974 was a crucial step for the entire Episcopalian-Anglican communion. There are now about 8,000 ordained women priests serving in most of the 38 churches worldwide. In 1988 a further step was taken when Barbara Harris was elected suffragan bishop in the Episcopalian diocese of Boston. In the following year Penny Jamieson was elected to head the diocese of Dunedin in the Anglican Church of New Zealand. Her election was followed in Canada by the election of Victoria Matthews as suffragan bishop of Toronto and later as head of the diocese of Edmonton. In 1993 the Church of England ordained its first women.

In 2002 the Episcopal Church of the United States ordained Carol Joy Gallagher as suffragan bishop for the diocese of Southern Virginia, and in 2006 Katherine Jefferts Schori was elected presiding bishop, becoming the first woman elected to lead a church in the global Anglican communion.

However, the acceptance of women bishops in the Anglican communion has been slow. The Anglican Church of Ireland has opened the door to the ordination of women as bishops but they have yet to elect anyone. The General Synod of the Australia Anglican Church in 2004 could not reach the required two-thirds majority vote from each of the Houses of Bishops, Clergy, and Laity to ordain women bishops. The synod held by the Scottish Episcopalian Church in Edinburgh in 2006 has moved to amend canon law in such a way that all references to the sex of a person would be removed from the conditions for election as a bishop. The Church of England, with a somewhat longer timetable, has begun efforts to see if legal elements could be reworked so that ordination of women as bishops might be possible by 2012.

Female Anglican priest in England breaking the communion bread during the Eucharist.

THREAT OF SCHISM

A similar challenge to the traditional nature of the priesthood and ministry has been raised in another area that is often linked to human rights. Just as women have claimed that their exclusion from the priesthood and from their election as bishops is unfair, so have gay men and women now brought forth a similar objection. This challenge has caused even more tension, since many Protestants interpret the Bible as teaching that homosexual conduct is inherently sinful. The discussion was intensified with the consecration of Eugene Robinson, an openly homosexual priest, as bishop of the New Hampshire diocese of the Episcopal Church in 2003.

The Episcopal Church in the United States is increasingly likely to split into two churches on this one issue. This affects not only the church in the United States but is now threatening the worldwide Anglican communion. In the eyes of traditionalists the Episcopal Church in the United States has broken away from "Apostolic teachings," while in the eyes of many within the Episcopal Church they are being true to the "Gospel of Love" of Jesus Christ. This division is one which will not easily be resolved and is in fact likely to lead to schism.

This consecration of homosexual priests has caused not only great debate within the Anglican/Episcopal Church, but has even brought threats of schism within the church body. This threat of schism has extended itself to the Evangelical Lutheran Church in America, which pleaded with its members "to find ways to live together faithfully in the midst of our disagreements." The church's current policy is to allow persons who are homosexual to be ordained as long as they maintain a lifestyle of celibacy. At its General Council meeting in 2005 a slim majority of members voted against a measure that would have allowed noncelibate gay ordination. The issue of gay priesthood is also linked to the consideration of marital unions between homosexual partners, another topic that is strongly debated in many Protestant churches, with similar fears of causing schisms. There are many indications that the road ahead for Protestantism will be a rocky one.

In the 20th century, faced with immediate problems associated with unchecked population growth, such as overcrowding and the danger of spoiling or depleting many of the earth's valuable natural resources, governments put considerable institutional force behind birth control. With the development of new birth control, or contraception methods, and the desire on the part of many people to limit the size of their families, new challenges have been posed to traditional moral positions of the Christian churches on this question.

For Protestants the issue of birth control is a very complicated one. In making ethical judgments of this kind, moral teachers indicate that it is important to take into account the impact contraception has on society's sexual morals. Does birth control by some individuals promote sexual license and keep love at a shallow level? Or does it reduce fear of pregnancy and thus allow the love between a couple to grow without other concerns? Does

Protesters against Planned Parenthood at a rally in Houston, Texas.

contraception foster a disrespect for life in the pursuit of selfish pleasure? Or does it take away tensions in relationships where economic conditions make pregnancy unadvisable? Do governments encourage birth control in cultures and social classes for which they have no respect in order to control undesired population? These and many more complicated questions enter into the debate on contraception. Questions have existed before concerning birth control, but with the new relatively safe and effective technologies and the growing influence that can be exercised by governments, these questions have intensified immensely for contemporary Christians.

ABORTION

Like the issue of birth control, the issue of abortion has taken on grand proportions in the latter part of the 20th century and the early 21st century, especially in the United States. Protestant perspectives on the abortion issue vary considerably. At one end of the spectrum there are the strong antiabortion voices that stress the fetus's right to life, and at the other extreme there are the abortion-on-demand voices that stress the woman's right and freedom to control her own body and its reproductive processes. There are many Protestant positions in between these two extremes, most of them have a certain degree of tolerance toward the idea of a woman's right to choose.

Each pregnancy is unique and is surrounded by its own complex set of issues. Not only religious but medical, economic, and social factors also come into play when a woman is faced with the choice of whether or not to have an abortion. Consequently a Protestant woman who is considering terminating an unwanted pregnancy must also consider these factors in light of her moral

Birth Control and the Protestant Churches

Although many governments actively encouraged the use of birth control, the entire Christian church remained against it until 1930. In that year the first significant break in this united Christian front against birth control occurred when the Lambeth Conference of the Anglican Church cautiously approved certain methods other than sexual abstinence to avoid parenthood. Between 1930 and 1958 the major Protestant churches all publicly abandoned the absolute prohibition against contraception. By 1959, when the World Council of Churches endorsed contraceptive practice, the Protestant consensus in its favor was very strong.

convictions. Her family, her partner, her doctor, and her priest or minister representing the moral wisdom of her church can provide guidance as she makes the decision. Still, as individuals struggle with the issue of abortion it remains a controversial issue for Christians in an ever more secularized world, with its continually developing medical technology.

INTELLIGENT DESIGN AND EVOLUTION

Not only are Protestants facing challenges to their moral teachings, but some of their basic beliefs are being undermined. The biblical belief in God as the creator of heaven and earth is, in the judgment of some Protestant scientists and religious thinkers, not only being ignored but actively challenged in classrooms where science is presented as giving a complete explanation of nature and life.

Many Protestant scholars have no difficulty with the scientific teaching of evolution. They see it as an explanation of natural reality that follows a particular method and as long as it abides by and is aware of the limitations of that method, it can be considered compatible with the biblical belief in creation. Other Protestant thinkers, however, assert that evolution is often taught as if it could give a complete account of nature and life, thus becoming antitheistic.

A movement called the Intelligent Design Network, which has arisen within the United States but is now working worldwide, and many of whose proponents are evangelical Protestants, has launched an effort to combat what it views as the antitheistic prejudices of the teaching of science. It has made appeals to a tradition of scientific explanation that is not antitheistic. Pre-Christian authors such as the third-century B.C.E. Greek philosopher Aristotle argued that the order or design found in nature could only be explained by an appeal to a cause beyond what is visible to us. Two hundred years later, Cicero, the Latin author of a book on the nature of the gods, argued that "the divine power is to be found in a principle of reason which pervades the whole of nature." Christian tradition, in the form especially of the writings of Thomas Aquinas, presented a teleological or design-type of argument for God's existence as the cause of the order or design of the universe.

RELIGION AND POLITICS

Many moral issues are often considered as exclusively individual moral questions. Today, however, such moral questions as contraception and abortion extend beyond the borders of private morality to include consideration of the social, economic, and political conditions that influence an individual's moral decisions. In these and other areas many Protestants have been moved to examine the social and economic conditions under which they live.

In the United States, the Protestant churches, in particular, have for over a century espoused the need to push for social and political reforms. Despite the separation of church and state and the prohibition of the establishment of any religion, the U.S. Constitution guarantees the right of religious bodies to state their positions in regard to public policy issues. Churches cannot constitutionally demand that their views be taken into account in any legislation, but they can use their influence to try to persuade others concerning the moral correctness of their social and political opinions and attempt to mold public policy.

A specifically American response to this has been the formation of the "Moral Majority" movement. Created in the 1970s by clergy such as Jerry Falwell and Pat Robinson, it had a powerful presence in the 1980s and 1990s with its message of conservative Republican values and opposition to many aspects of contemporary secular culture.

Intelligent Design

The Intelligent Design Network has recently attempted to have its explanation of the order in nature and in the natural processes of life introduced as an alternative scientific explanation in some school districts in the United States. So far these efforts have been rejected by courts. In late 2005 a federal court found in *Kitzmiller v. Dover Area School District* that intelligent design as an explanation of the origin of life is not a scientific theory but based in religious belief, and that its teaching in public schools thus violated the First Amendment of the U.S. Constitution, which calls for the separation of church and state.

The movement backed certain political candidates and lobbied Congress and the White House in order to further its moral political agenda. Efforts on the part of such Christian groups are frequently judged by secularists to be extreme and disrespectful of the rights of people to live life as they choose. In recent years its power has waned, not least because of the rise of the evangelical environmental movement, which finds itself taking the side of many secular organizations in seeking to protect the natural world.

When strong religious and political forces combine there often results such strong conviction of rightness that objective discussion of issues can be diminished. Moderation and toleration can give way to fanaticism when religion and politics mix.

Members of a congregation of a Protestant church in Brandenburg, Germany, gather to protest against a nearby field of genetically modified corn.

When people feel threatened by the intensity of this conviction, as they often do, they tend not only to oppose the political positions associated with these groups, but also the churches that have become too identified with those positions. Most religious movements, however, have not taken on fanatical form. For the most part they continue to make valuable contributions to the moral, social, and political debates that take place in democracies every day.

CONCLUSION

Some aspects of Protestant Christianity, particularly in the United States, see themselves as currently under siege by secularism. Other Protestant churches are seeking to respond positively to these same challenges. The many continuing activities of the Protestant churches in today's world—their life of prayer, their many forms of renewal, their charismatic revivals, their reawakening in eastern Europe, their growth in Africa, their new commitments in South and Central America, and their ecumenical generosity—suggest that the promise of Christ at the end of Matthew's Gospel is still being fulfilled: "Go therefore and make disciples of all the nations . . . and lo, I am with you always, even to the end of the age." (Matthew 28:19–20)

FACT FILE

Worldwide Numbers
There are approximately 750 million Protestants (including Episcopalians, Lutherans, Presbyterians, Christian Scientists, Jehovah's Witnesses, and Mormons).

Holy Symbol
The cross on which Jesus was executed (crucified).

Holy Writings
The Bible, consisting of the Old Testament of Judaism originally written in Hebrew, and the New Testament, originally written in Greek.

Holy Places
Pilgrimage sites include Wittenburg in Germany, Canterbury in England, and Salt Lake City and Pennsylvania in the United States; also places in Israel, such as Bethlehem, because of their links with the life of Jesus.

Founders
Christianity, including Protestantism, Catholicism, and Orthodoxy, is named after Jesus of Nazareth—called "Christ" from the Greek word for "chosen one", who was crucified in about 29 C.E. Protestantism was founded in the 16th century in Germany by Martin Luther and others who "protested" at the faults they saw in the Catholic Church.

Festivals
Christmas, celebrating the birth of Jesus Christ (December 25); Easter, marking his death and resurrection (March–April); Ascension Day, celebrating his return to heaven (May), and Pentecost, which celebrates the coming of the Holy Spirit to his disciples (May–June).

BIBLIOGRAPHY

Bates, Katharine Lee. *America the Beautiful*. New York: Scholastic, 2001.

Cochrane, Arthur C. *Reformed Confessions of the 16th Century*. Louisville, Ky: Westminster John Knox Press, 2003.

Eddy, Mary Baker. *Science and Health with Key to the Scriptures*. Boston, Mass: Christian Science Board of Directors, 1994.

Eliot, T. S. *Complete Poems and Plays*. New York: Harcourt, Brace, 1952.

Luther, Martin, Harold John Grimm, and Leo. *Christian Liberty*. Philadelphia: Fortress Press, 1957.

Marvell, Andrew, and Nigel Smith. *Marvell: The Poems of Andrew Marvell*. Longman annotated English poets. Harlow: Longman, 2003.

Milton, John, and F. T. Prince. *Paradise Lost: Books I and II*. London: Oxford University Press, 1962.

FURTHER READING

Brackney, William H. *Historical Dictionary of the Baptists.* Lanham, Md: Scarecrow Press, 2009.

Breuilly, Elizabeth, Martin Palmer, Martin E. Marty, and Joanne O'Brien. *Religions of the World: The Illustrated Guide to Origins, Beliefs, Traditions & Festivals.* Gisborne, Vic: Alto Books, 2007.

Carroll, Anthony J. *Protestant Modernity: Weber, Secularization, and Protestantism.* Scranton, Pa: University of Scranton Press, 2008.

Griffith, Bill. *By Faith Alone: One Family's Epic Journey Through 400 Years of American Protestantism.* New York: Harmony Books, 2007.

Mead, Frank Spencer, Samuel S. Hill, Craig D. Atwood, and Frank Spencer Mead. *Handbook of Denominations in the United States.* Nashville: Abingdon Press, 2005.

McKeever, Bill, and Eric Johnson. *Mormonism 101: Examining the Religion of the Latter-Day Saints.* Grand Rapids, Mich: Baker Books, 2000.

Muray, Leslie A. *Liberal Protestantism and Science.* Greenwood guides to science and religion. Westport, Conn: Greenwood Press, 2008.

Nestingen, James Arne. *Martin Luther: A Life.* Minneapolis, MN: Augsburg Books, 2003.

O'Brien, Joanne, Martin Palmer, and Joanne O'Brien. *The Atlas of Religion.* Berkeley: University of California Press, 2007.

Tavard, George Henry. *The Starting Point of Calvin's Theology.* Grand Rapids, Mich. [u.a.]: Eerdmans, 2000.

Westerfield Tucker, Karen B. *American Methodist Worship.* Oxford: Oxford University Press, 2001.

WEB SITES

Further facts and figures, history, and current status of the religion can be found on the following Web sites:

http://protestant.christianityinview.com
This Web site provides a short introduction to and history of Protestantism, exploring its multi-faceted nature, development, and modern practises.

http://www.oikoumene.org/
The Web site of the World Council of Churches. It looks at and provides information on all aspects of Christianity, so here Protestantism is seen in context with other Christian denominations.

www.religion-online.org
Religion Online is designed to assist teachers, scholars, and general "seekers" who are interested in exploring religious issues.

www.religioustolerance.org/christ7.htm
The Christianity section of a very comprehensive and informative Web site about world religions. This site sets out to provide accurate, balanced, clear, objective, and inclusive articles about religion, morality and ethics, and has tackled tough religious questions. It does not promote a specific religious viewpoint, nor does it attack anyone's theological beliefs.

GLOSSARY

apostle—One of the 12 disciples chosen by Jesus (Matthew 2:4) or one of certain other early Christian leaders. (Acts 14:14; Romans 16:7; Galatians 1:1)

Assyria—One of the strong Middle East civilizations that conquered the Jewish people in 731 B.C.E.

Babylonia—One of the conquering nations that overcame the Jewish people. They flourished in the Mesopotamian area and conquered the Jews in 586 B.C.E.

baptism—Ceremony in which one enters the church family. It is a way of showing that you have been washed free of sin by the death and rising from the dead of Jesus Christ.

basilica—A church such as the Lateran Basilica, built according to an ancient Roman plan for a court of justice or a place of public assembly, with an oblong nave and a semicircular apse at one end.

beatitudes—The blessings listed by Jesus in his Sermon on the Mount. They are considered the equivalent to the Ten Commandments of Moses or the expectations of the ideals to be pursued by Christians.

catechism—A textbook regarding Christian beliefs and life used for preparing believers to accept the responsibilities of mature faith.

charismatic—Gifted with charisma or spiritual grace, particularly one of the manifestations of the Holy Spirit, such as speaking in tongues.

charismatic movement—A religious movement, begun as Pentecostalism in the United States in 1901, that accentuates personal and direct experience of the Holy Spirit independently of sacraments and church institutions.

chrism—Holy Oil blessed for confirmation and symbolizing the strength that is necessary for leading a mature Christian life and facing the challenges the call to Christian maturity brings.

church—The people of God or those destined to inherit the kingdom of God.

creed—A short statement of the basic beliefs of the Christian church (e.g., the Apostles' Creed, the Athanasian Creed, and the Nicene Creed).

ecumenism—From the Greek *oikoumene,* "the whole inhabited world." Any attempts to deal with the relations between different Christian groups or to think of ways in which divisions might be overcome.

Eucharist—The sacrament whereby the bread and wine really or symbolically become the body and blood of Christ.

excommunication—The formal cutting off of a person from the life of the church and the reception of the sacraments.

fathers of the church—Early church authors (e.g., Ambrose, Jerome, Augustine, Basil, Gregory of Nyssa) who explained the scriptures with great acuity and whose writings thus gained authority within the church community.

Final Judgment—In contrast to the particular judgment given at death, this is the time, at Christ's Second Coming, when the fate of human beings will be decided for all eternity.

hymn—A religious poem set to music and sung as part of worship.

iconostasis—A screen, ornamented with rows of icons, that separates the nave from the altar in many Eastern churches. It is beyond this screen that the bread and wine are transformed into the body and blood of Christ during the Divine Liturgy.

incarnation—The mystery believed by Christians that God became man by the union of the divine and human natures in the person of Jesus Christ.

indulgence—The removal in full or in part of the punishment due for sins. Even after sins have been forgiven through the sacrament of penance and true contrition, sinners still owe some form of recompense for the sins they have committed.

infallibility—The belief held by Roman Catholics that the pope cannot make an error in matters of faith and morals when he speaks by virtue of his office.

Messiah—An anointed king promised to the Jewish people as someone who would lead them to overcome their enemies. Messiah, in Hebrew, means "anointed one." The corresponding word in Greek is *Christos* or, in English, "Christ."

monk—A religious man following the Rule who spends most of his day in prayer and who attempts to lead a perfect Christian life by taking vows pledging himself to poverty, chastity, and obedience.

Pentecost—The feast celebrated by Christian believers in May or June commemorating Christ's sending of the Holy Spirit to the apostles. It is considered by Christians to be the birthday of the church.

Pharisee—The Hebrew for "separatist." One of a group of observant Jews, beginning before the time of Jesus and continuing with important leadership roles afterward. The Pharisees helped develop an elaborate system of oral laws to apply the written Law of Moses to Jewish life after the Roman conquest of their homeland and the destruction of the Temple.

Protestant—A term first used in 1529 to express the protest of several princes and representatives of 14 German cities against an attempt by the Roman Catholic emperor Charles V to limit the practice of Lutheranism within the Holy Roman Empire. The term later was extended to Lutherans and other Christians who separated from Roman Catholicism.

resurrection—The belief that Christ rose from the dead after his crucifixion and death. It is the guarantee, according to Saint Paul, that the followers of Christ will similarly survive physical death and be joined with their heavenly Father.

sacraments—Signs of divine help or grace needed for living a good Christian life, through which God confers the help of grace he promises.

Sadducee—A member of the priestly family who believed in the religious authority of the Torah, or first five books of the Bible alone, and who opposed the new interpretations advanced by the Pharisees.

schism—A split between two churches that does not involve the denial of any truth of the faith. Such a denial of a truth of the Christian faith would be called heresy.

scribes—The learned class among the Jews and the official authorities on the written law and the oral traditions. The function of the priests was to care for ceremonies; the function of the scribes was to clarify doctrine or teaching. Generally the scribes sided with the Pharisees rather than the Sadducees.

Second Vatican Council—A worldwide church council for Roman Catholics opened by Pope John XXIII in 1962 for bringing Roman Catholic life and teaching up to date. Vatican II was closed by Pope Paul VI in 1965.

seminary—A school for training members of the clergy or those who exercise the role of leader's in churches.

Trinity—The Christian belief that in God there are three persons: the Father, the Son (who became man in Christ), and the Holy Spirit.

vernacular—Local language permitted to be used in religious ceremonies instead of the official Latin and Greek languages that had been used by Roman Catholics and Orthodox churches for centuries.

INDEX

ABOUT THE AUTHOR

Stephen F. Brown is chairperson of the theology department at Boston College. He has edited several volumes on medieval philosophy and theology, including *Philosophical Writings* by William of Ockham and *On Faith and Reason* by St. Thomas Aquinas.

ABOUT THE SERIES EDITORS

Martin Palmer is the founder of ICOREC (International Consultancy on Religion, Education, and Culture) in 1983 and is the secretary-general of the Alliance of Religions and Conservation (ARC). He is the author of several books on world religions.

Joanne O'Brien has an M.A. degree in Theology and has written a range of educational and general reference books on religion and contemporary culture. She is co-author, with Martin Palmer and Elizabeth Breuilly, of *Religions of the World* and *Festivals of the World* published by Facts On File Inc.

PICTURE CREDITS